MW01610331

The

Effects

of DIVORCE

on CHILDREN

A Mother-Son Perspective

DEBORAH A. HENADY-KORBA

LifeRich Publishing is a registered trademark of The Reader's Digest Association, Inc.

LifeRich Publishing books may be ordered through booksellers or by contacting:

LifeRich Publishing
1663 Liberty Drive
Bloomington, IN 47403
www.liferichpublishing.com
1 (888) 238-8637

ISBN: 978-1-4897-1218-9 (sc)
ISBN: 978-1-4897-1219-6 (hc)
ISBN: 978-1-4897-1217-2 (e)

Library of Congress Control Number: 2017904354

Print information available on the last page.

LifeRich Publishing rev. date: 04/14/2017

Dedicated to
Our Lord, God
and
My late Husband, Jerome
who was always supportive

ABSTRACT

In examining the effects of post- divorce adjustment of boys 8-12 years of age and how divorce impacts their development using Erikson's psychosocial stages of development as a basis for understanding this adjustment. The problem is that there is very little research related to adjustment issues in boys in the age group following divorce. The purpose of this critical literature review is to establish connections with divorce and a number of issues related to adjustment including problem solving skills, coping mechanisms, attachment and bonding, explanatory style, vulnerability, resilience, risk, and adjustment problems with behavioral and emotional outcomes.

The findings of the present research suggest that boys experience increased stress leading to decreased adaptation and ineffective coping skills, both of which have the potential to lead to health issues and interference with their psychosocial developmental process (with divorce serving as a catalyst for adjustment difficulties). Present research findings suggest that there is no specific decline in the relationship between a mother and son following divorce; however, the evidence suggests that boys may display more aggressive acting-out behaviors following the divorce of the parents. A model is proposed that is based upon the psychological diathesis-stress model and includes a more holistic approach to understanding the impact of stressors that includes protective (resiliency) and risk factors.

Further investigations are needed in addressing the possible impacts of the explanatory style relating to coping, defense mechanisms, and resiliency. Future research is strongly suggested to answer questions regarding how children's adjustment is impacted in non-traditional families (e.g. families headed by gay, lesbian, transsexual, and bisexual parents and non-traditional divorced families) and the existence of gender differences related to the impact of divorce on males and females? It is proposed that the modified diathesis-stress model could be used by therapists as an intervention assessment tool.

TABLE OF CONTENTS

CHAPTER 1

INTRODUCTION TO THE LITERATURE REVIEW

Problem Statement

The problem of the present critical review focuses on the impact of divorce adjustment experience by boys 8-12 years-of-age, the influences on their developmental stage, and the mother-son relationship. What is needed is an understanding of the links between boys' problem solving skills, coping mechanisms, behavioral and emotional outcomes, and divorce. Current studies of coping behaviors among boys have led to several research questions. How do boys' between the ages of 8-12 in divorced families cope successfully? What are their coping behaviors? Is there a relationship between the effects of post- divorce adjustment on boys who are between 8 and 12 years of age and their developmental stages leading to increased behavioral and emotional problems? What are the effects of post- divorce adjustment on the mother-son relationship?

To answer these questions, investigative studies on the coping behaviors and developmental levels of boys between the ages of 8 and 12 years old in divorced families must be examined. A research problem can be found in the design of prior investigations in that this research leaves out consideration of gender as well as the development stage. There is a lack of differentiation between the coping behaviors of boys and girls and the link to the child's developmental stage. Focus on a research design that incorporates a developmental theory is appropriate in the study of the coping behaviors among boys in families that have experienced divorce.

Purpose

The purposes of this critical review are two-fold. First, it is important to discover the patterns of coping behaviors in boys between the ages of 8 and 12 from families that have experienced divorce. Second, the literature will be reviewed to determine the impact of divorce and developmental stages of the boys in the age group of 8 to 12 years of age and the mother-son relationship. The developmental stages to be explore (but not limited to) will include trust versus mistrust, industry versus inferiority, and identity versus identity diffusion.

Rationale for the Study

Boys and girls between the ages of 8-12 need to be encouraged and guided to utilize effective coping skills. During this critical time period in their lives with confusion and self-exploration, boys are faced with all types of decisions and choices about themselves (Allen, 1995). Ineffective coping skills may lead to decisions that would negatively impact the remainder of their lives (Luther, Burack, Cincchetti, & Weisz, 1997). These negative external behaviors may lead to difficulties with peers, the law, school, drug/alcohol abuse, deviant sexual behaviors, delinquency, and relationship problems with the opposite sex. These problems when left unresolved may follow boys into manhood and plague them long after they become adults (Forman, 1993; Hetherington & Blechman, 1996). By identifying coping skills among boys between the ages of 8-12 whose families have experienced divorce- this study can add to the paucity of data about the coping skills of boys. Too much of the literature relates only to girls or does not differentiate coping skills by gender.

Children and adolescents from divorced families' experience more adjustment problems than children growing up in nuclear families (Simons, Lin, Gordon, Conger, & Lorenz, 1999). The trend toward using developmentally appropriate practices have been linked to their ability to cope with anger, distress, how they understand their feelings, and their behavior (Denhan, 1998). According to Greene and Leslie (1989), boys from divorced families were found to experience difficulties in schoolwork. They also exhibited greater stress and higher levels of aggression than did boys from nuclear families. In an extensive literature review of the databases of THOR, ERIC, PSYCHLIT, SCIENCE ACCESS, EBSCO, and various other Walden databases, results have indicated boys from divorced families exhibit external aggressiveness, while girls tend to internalize their emotions (e.g., Amato, 1993; Alexander, Waldron, Barton, & Mas, 1989; Biller, 1981; Bowlby, 1980; Capaldi & Patterson, 1991; Clarke-Stewart, Vandell, McCartney, Owen, & Booth, 2000; Cohen-Sadler,

Berman, & King, 1982; Emery & O'Leary, 1982; Erkison, 1968; Froman, 1993; Forgatch, Patterson, & Skinner, 1998; Howell, Portes, & Brown, 1997; Jenkins & Smith, 1993; Luthar, Burack, Cincchetti, & Weiss, 1997; Martinez& Forgatch, 2002; Olweus, 1980; Rutter, 1990; Sun, 2001p; Wallerstein & Kelly, 1980; Woodward, Fergusson, & Belsky, 2000; Zaslow, 1988; Zill, Morrison, & Coiro, 1993).

Theoretical Framework

Underlying the behavior discussed in the previous section is attachment theory and Erikson's psychosocial developmental theory. Both theories provide a solid framework and foundation for this investigation and literature review. The findings from several studies are consistent; children have been found to disengage from the family when parents' divorce. Dishion (1987) and Snyder, Dishion, and Patterson (1986) found an association between diminished parenting, child adjustment problems, and the increased risk for membership/association in deviant peer groups (Capaldi & Patterson, 1991). Adjustment problems include antisocial behavior, drug use, peer rejection, deviant peer association, poor academic achievement, low self-esteem, and depression.

It is commonly believed among researchers that personality is influenced by affective events that take place during formative periods of development in infancy and childhood (Allen & Bell, 1995; Clark-Stewart, Vandell, McCartney, Owen, & Booth, 2000). Many developmental researchers have viewed the relationships between children and parents as important for shaping interpersonal behavior competencies and personality. Attachment theory was first proposed because of children's experiences with parents during early childhood and pre-adolescent becomes internalized as cognitive representations (Bowlby, 1958; 1969; 1973; 1980). These experiences shape children's perceptions of themselves and serve as templates for subsequent interpersonal relationships. They also direct and manage their perceptions in a broad range of situations and over the entire course of the lifespan.

The chief proponent of development theory was Erikson (1959, 1968). According to his view of psychosocial development, a child progresses through developmental stages by resolving conflicts that arise from a need to adapt to the sociocultural environment (Lefrancois, 1990). The core of the process is the gradual acquisitions of an ego identity-that is, a strong sense of personal worth and integrity. At each development stage are basic tasks that must be mastered if the individual is to achieve normal development and a healthy adjustment. Failure to perform any of these tasks may impede development in succeeding stages.

The stages of Erikson that are the focus of the present critical literature review include trust versus mistrust, industry versus inferiority, and identity versus role diffusion. These tasks must be addressed at the middle childhood stage of development (between ages 6 and 12). During these stages of development the child is expanding his or her knowledge and understanding of the social and physical world. The child is also building confidence and self-esteem (Erikson, 1968; 1980). When dissention within the family occurs, a greater level of stress and conflict is created. The stress and conflict occurring during this critical time period may inhibit the boy's resolutions of the psychosocial developmental stages. This conflict may be exacerbated by societies stereotypical standards (e.g. boys that cry are sissies, males are to be macho and strong, males do not exhibit emotions for this is a sign of weakness). These early stages of development are key elements in the mother-son relationship of bonding and attachment, discipline measures, interactions, and maternal support.

Background and Topic Analysis

In many western countries, there has been a substantial rise in the number of marriages ending in separation and divorce (Woodward, Fergusson, & Belsky, 2000). Since 1958, there were 2.1 divorces per 1,000 with a steady increase reaching 2.5 per 1,000 in 1965. During 1979 through 1981 divorce increased by 5.3 per 1,000 and by 1984 one out of every two marriages ended in divorce (Glick, Lin, 1986; Shaw, Emery, & Tuer, 1993). By 1985 divorce affected approximately one million children a year in the United States and 100,000 per year in Canada living in single-parent homes (Fine, 1987).

During the 1990's, the divorce rate began to decrease, however in 2000 it was estimated that 20 million children under the age of 18 lived with only one parent. Of these 20 million children, 72% lived with their mother, 16% were shared in joint custody, and 9% lived with their fathers (the remaining 3% had undetermined custodial status).

One explanation that has been offered is that boys have a more difficult time in adjusting to divorce because of the father's absence (Amato, 1993; Hetherington and Blechman, 1996; Hetherington and Parke, 1979). The focus over the past two decades has been directed more towards the custodial parent or the father-daughter relationship. Many questions still remain today relating divorce effects and children's adjustment problems with the absence of one parent, while leaving the responsibility on the parent rearing the children. In examining the literature of the mother-son relationship within the two-year time frame following parental divorce, a look at boy's coping mechanisms has not been adequately explored. Yet the importance of the topic is clear. All of the areas of a boy's life are intertwined with the child's ability to cope with the situation and the utilization of effective coping skills, which impact the boy's psychosocial development.

Interpersonal socialization factors play a role in the development of a child's coping abilities (Forman, 1993). Interpersonal socialization factors come from parents and other important individuals in a child's life. Children learn most of their socialization skills from their parents during the critical stages of early development (Hetherington & Blechman, 1996). Parents that react to their children with encouragement, positive emotional expression, understanding, and comfort provide a positive social learning environment. This environment provides positive modeling to the children, teaching them effective coping skills. Parents that respond to their children with anger, rage, physical, psychological, or emotional abuse, hinder the child's ability to learn positive coping skills needed for stressful life events. The social learning provided through this type of modeling is only encouraging aggressive negative behaviors and defiance.

The disruption during the boy's developmental stages may be the first critical variable affecting the post-divorce adjustment of boys. A second critical variable to be explored is the impact of stress and conflict added to boys during the post-divorce adjustment phase, which lead to disruption during the psychosocial developmental stages creating ineffective coping skills for boys' ages 8-12. It would seem that this state of turmoil especially impacts the mother-son relationship. These two variables may be found to interact and subsequently determine much about the process of the boys' adaptation, adjustment, and responses to their environment both internally and externally. Again, the importance of the review lies in addressing these particular areas as well.

Just as divorce is known to be a stressful situation for adults, it is equally if not more stressful for children (Amato, 1993; Wallerstein & Kelly, 1980). There are many stressful factors surrounding a divorce, including the loss of parent/ grandparents, internal conflict, decreased standard of living, moving change of school, and negative societal stereotypes. Other conditions that can follow divorce include depression, decreased self-esteem, and stress (Allen, Hauser, O'Connor, Bell, & Eickholt, 1996; Booth & Amato, 1994). Stress is the process by which environmental events challenge or threaten us, how those events are interpreted, how they make us feel, and how we respond and adjust to them (Baum, Gatchel, & Krantz, 1997). The stress process is a necessary part of the human adaption. There must be a balance with in the human organism for maintaining homeostasis between the internal and external environmental stressors. A little stress is needed in human life, however if there is too much stress in one's life it may become harmful to the body and lead to decrease in the functioning of the immune system, which in turn leads to disease processes that damage the organism (Turks & Bellisimo, 1990). Too much stress such as that which could occur from parents who are divorcing can lead to acting out and negative behaviors in the young child in his or her effort to cope. Whereas much of the literature focuses on the child's reaction, only some of the studies assess these reactions in terms of gender and even fewer studies specifically concentrate on boys between the ages of 8-12.

Topic Importance and Usefulness

The contribution of this study is to increase the knowledge about divorce and young children, especially the impact upon boys. A few years ago at a conference sponsored by the United States national Institute of child Health and Human Development (NICHD) was held to evaluate existing knowledge about how children are affected by parental divorce. In closing the participants of the conference prepared a statement suggestion that what was needed next was a longitudinal investigation of the large sample of children from intact families. This investigation was to commence before the parents' were divorced, providing the effects of pre-and post-disruption circumstances which could be separated (Lamb et al., 1999).

Following the conference, a study was performed by Clarke-Stewart, Vandell, McCartney, Owen, & Booth in 2000. What they found were differences do exist both before marital separation and after marital separation in mothers' circumstances and characteristics related to family structure and marital status, both were found to be significant and sizable. After the separation it was found that incomes were lower, depression levels increased, mothers were found to work more hours per week. The child (ren) were provide with less support and stimulation. These findings were consistent with those of research on mothers of older children, which showed that compared with married mothers, single and separated or divorced mothers not only are poorer (Bianchi, 1995; Emery, 1998) but suffer more depression and anxiety (Lamb et al., 1999; Pett et al., 1999) and are less capable as parents (Karr & Easley, 1986; MacKinnon et al., 1982, 1986; Pett et al., 1999; Weinraub & Gringlas, 1995).

As previously noted, the major question of the literature review relates to the mother-son relationship following divorce and the impact on boys' adjustment. According to one study, boys of divorced parents experience more adjustment problems than those who grow up in nuclear families (Simon, Lin, Gordon, Conger, & Lorenz, 1999). According to the literature, research studies implicated paternal divorce as an immediate and major factor of disruption in the lives of boys (Capaldi & Patterson, 1991; Clarke-Stewart et al., 2000; Martinez & Forgatch, 2002; Sun, 2001). These disruptions lead to changes related to the social, cognitive, and emotional development of boys (Biller, 1981; Emery, Hetherington, & DiLalla, 1984; Garvin, Leber, & Kalter, 1991; Guidubaldi & Perry, 1985; Wallerstein & Kelly, 1980). Another area that has been overlooked directly is the effect upon boys' physical health as related to the psychosocial developmental stage conflict that has been increased by the stress of divorce. According to Emery and O'Leary (1982), marital discord can be seen as a precursor of childhood disorders and the initial beginning of developmental psychopathology. The importance of the present critical review also lay therefore in providing more information in this area by examining the literature related to the impact of divorce on boys ages 8 through 12 and by including developmental theory as a possible variable of significance.

Clearly, these disruptions have an impact upon boy's development stages including positive or negative coping skills, relationships with their parents, and ultimately a strong impact upon their health and psychological well-being. What is not known, however, is to what degree they disrupt the boys' development, how this disruption impacts the mother-son relationship, what coping skills boys can employ to counteract this disruption, and what interventions can be identified to enhance their coping abilities. The importance of the study lies with adding to this paucity of data. The study is thus significant to all fields of Psychology with a stronger influence in the areas of Developmental, Abnormal, Health, Counseling, and Marriage & Family.

The usefulness of the present literature review relates to the fact that this researcher was only able to find a few current studies on the subject of the effects of divorce on children as it relates to boys. The literature that is reviewed in this investigative study is dated. The integration of these studies with up to date knowledge clearly lends importance to the present research with an indication that more research is needed in this area. This is further supported by the NICHD study where it was found that boys were more affected in terms of cognitive performance with a display of negative behaviors with their mothers. It was observed that boy's were more affected than girls by their parents' divorce (Hetherington et al., 1979, 1982; Howell et al., 1997; Jenkins & Smith, 1993; Mott et al., 1997; Simons, 1996; Wallerstein & Blakeslee, 1989; Wallerstein & Kelly, 1980; Zaslow, 1988), particularly in the areas of social adjustment and mother-child relationships (Amato & Keith, 1991).

Assumptions

With regard to assumptions, this researcher assumed that the studies included in the critical literature review were a representative sample of the larger body of research that currently exists on the impact of post-divorce adjustment on boys 8-12 years-of-age, the influences of their developmental stage, and the mother-son relationship. Interpretive analysis from a presentation of the literature engenders certain assumptions. The researcher will report the findings as related to the topic.

Five of the most frequently found variables were increased guilt, decreased sociability, increased withdrawal, increased depression, and decreased self-confidence (Peretti & DiVitorrio, 1992). These assumptions included but are not limited to mother and father depression predicts child's depression (especially daughters), mother's sensitivity predicts child's sensitivity, father's lack of sensitivity predicted son's submissiveness (Burns & Dunlop, 2003). A father's absence from the home is associated with a greater decline in the quality of the home environment for boys (Mott et al., 1997) and a negative influence linked with child misbehaviors. The link of family disruption and the father's absence has the greatest impact during the post-divorce adjustment (Santrock, 1972). The father's absence creates less investment on the part of the son towards either parent (Burns & Dunlop, 2003) creating long term negative effects (Orbuch, Thornton, & Cancio, 2000).

The value society places on boys and the role fathers play in the socialization of children impacts a strong relationship between fatherlessness and social problems (Machey & Coney, 2000). These problems along with disrupted parenting practices mediate relationships between emotional adjustment and maladaptive behaviors, which may lead to psychopathology (Forgatch & DeGarmo, 2002; Martinez & Forgatch, 2002). Sons' will often lose their male identification object (father) at the time of their own identity development, which creates grave distress (Schalin, 1983). This distress increases with the changing family structure, disrupted roles, and relationships all create less social supports and increased stressful life events. The stress may become so overwhelming that the boy will turn to social risk taking behaviors.

Bearss (1941) performed a study at the State Prison for Southern Michigan at Jackson involving 500 inmates. It was revealed in the study that 80% of the prisoners came from broken homes and 43% of these males had been juvenile delinquents with court records (Bearss, 1941). A strong suggestion has been posed that there could be an association between parental loss and juvenile delinquency (Borduin & Henggeler, 1987; Pitt-Aikens & McKinnon, 2000). Indicating boys of divorced parents are more likely to become involved in more risk taking deviant behaviors e.g. engaging in sexual activity at younger ages and more frequently than boys of intact families) (Whitbeck, Simons, & Meei-Ying, 1994). This notion is particularly contingent upon the mother –son relationship. Single mother households are more aware of their mother's dating, sexual behaviors and attitudes, which are all used in the re-establishment of her own sociability. These adult attitudes and behaviors may be disturbing for the children, for this is the time when they are discovering their own sexual identity and development. Many of these developmental issues being discovered include identity, sexuality, sociability, body image, self-esteem, peer pressure, and effective coping skills; while many of the same issues their mother is revisiting in her adulthood (Whitbeck, Simons, & Meei-Ying, 1994).

Wallerstein & Resnikoff (1997) revealed through clinical observations children in the first 3 years of life develop an internalized template of good relationships, which enable them to turn away from disappointment related to parents and the invest their energies in school, friends, and others. The other relationships help the child to propel himself forward at each point of development into the next developmental stage, moving increasingly away from his family towards increased independence, competence, and resiliency (Wallerstein & Resnikoff, 1997).

Limitations and Delimitations

It is important to note that the present critical literature review was limited by that amount of information and data discovered in the documents, reports, and studies comprising the literature review. The conclusions of the study were also subjected to the same limitation. In addition, an inherent limitation may exist. There could be unknown research and documentation not taken into consideration by this researcher that might significantly influence conclusions. However, as Creswell (2003) has noted, similar limitations inhibit the validation of findings of any study or research project.

The investigation research was also limited by use of a critical literature review methodology only and did not include a survey or other validated instruments to collect the data. The delimitations of the study are related to gender and age. The study focused on boys between the ages of 8-12. Triangulation of information- that is, the use of several different forms of data collected through both qualitative and quantitative approach – is the strongest type of research (Creswell, 2003).

Of the greatest importance was the fact that the current literature review findings were derived mostly from older investigative research and empirical studies. Many of the studies targeted girls' responses and coping related to parental divorce. The articles addressing divorce effects and boys' were found to be related to adjustment problems (Borduin & Henggeler, 1987; Emery & O'Leary, 1982; Forgatch et al., 1996; Martinez & Forgatch, 2002), aggressive behaviors (Mackey, 2000; Olweus, 1980), antisocial behaviors (Forgatch et al., 1998; Pitt-Aikens & McKinnon, 2000), the importance of the father-son relationship (Katzev et al., 1994; Orbuch et al., 2000; Schalin, 1983), parental transitions and parenting practices (Burns & Dunlop, 2002; Capaldi & Patterson, 1991; Forgatch & DeGarmo, 2002; Martinez & Forgatch, 2002), gender differences (Burns & Dunlop, 2001; Koerner et al., 2004; Mott et al., 1997), and resiliency and development

(Hetherington & Blechman, 1996; Masten et al., 1990). Thus the findings of the present study were limited to results mainly concluded over the past 10-25 years.

Transitional Statement

Thus far this review has described the problem of the study and the purpose of the study, explained the rationale and theoretical framework, and discussed the topic analysis, background, and topic importance and usefulness. Included also were descriptions of the study assumptions as well as limitations and delimitations. It was noted in the first chapter that the stress experienced by boys during divorce adjustment might create decreased adaption to their current situation and the environment. The increased amounts of stress and the inner turmoil may lead to a decreased state of health and ineffective coping skills. The ineffective coping skills and stress may lead to unresolved health issues (real or imagined) creating interference with the psychosocial developmental process. Thus, in this context stress impacts the process of adaption and adjustment, as well as the child's coping skills.

In Chapter 2, the literature will review the impact of divorce on the mother-son relationship, which includes many articles and theories with reference to stress and health, psychosocial stages of development, and theories of bonding and attachment. These are reviewed and discussed in depth in an effort to acquire information to answer the research questions. Also included in this section are studies pertinent to vulnerability, risk, resilience, and the Diathesis-Stress Model.

In Chapter 3, the Integrated Summary of the Literature, provides data regarding current gaps in the research, concludes the findings on the impact of divorce on boys, and recommends the use of a revised Diathesis-Stress Model to include protective factors and risk factors. Other recommendations are also included. Contributions to new knowledge are discussed as well.

CHAPTER 2

IMPACT OF POST DIVORCE ADJUSTMENT ON YOUNG BOYS

Introduction and Use of Related Literature

The following chapter will discuss the impact of divorce upon one's stress and health and how this effects a person's adaptation with a review of Seyle's (1976) GAS Theory and Seligman's (1992) Explanatory Style. Stress, coping resiliency, and coping intervention skills are important and interact with one's developmental stage(s). A review of Erikson's (1959, 1968, 1980) Psychosocial Stages of Development will also be included with a closer look at stages of trust verses mistrust, industry verses inferiority, and identity verses identity diffusion. Marcia's (1966) stage of identity diffusion will also be examined. All of these areas of development are impacted when an adolescent experiences the divorce of one's parents. Theories of attachment and bonding will be explored briefly from each of the following views: psychoanalytic, psychosocial, learning, social learning, ethological, and ecological because all of these theories have made a contribution towards the importance of the parent/child bond. The emotional bonds of attachment are strong motivators in children's behavior, which impact their vulnerability, risk, resiliency, and their coping abilities, all of which become crucial factors when an adolescent is faced with parental divorce. Many of these factors have reciprocal interactions. Following the review described above, the diathesis-stress model is presented with the addition of risk and protective factors as related to divorce, followed by a conclusion and summary of results.

The literature review included an extensive search of the databases of THOR, ERIC, PSYCHLIT, SCIENCE ASSCESS, EBSCO, and various Walden databases. A number of key terms searched in the databases included, but were not limited to: Seyle's GAS Theory of Stress; Seligman's Explanatory Style; Erikson's Psychosocial stages, identity versus identity diffusion; Marcia's Developmental Theory; Theories of attachment and bonding; Psychoanalytic, Psychosocial, Learning, Social Learning, Ethological, Ecological; effects of divorce on children, children and divorce, divorce effects, divorce, parental divorce, effects of divorce on health, boys ages 8-12 of divorce, mother and son relationship, impacts of divorce, children's explanatory style, divorce and psychopathology, defense mechanisms, risk, resiliency, vulnerability, attachment, bonding, mother & son attachment & bonding, boys' adjustment & divorce, juvenile delinquency, stress & health, coping, coping interventions, coping mechanisms, and the Diathesis-Stress Model. One of the greatest important factors of the current literature review was the findings were derived mostly from older investigative studies, literature reviews, and empirical data.

Many of the studies targeted girls' responses and coping related to parental divorce while making assumptions about how boys react and cope. Many of the current studies were found to address adult children of divorce. Thus, the findings of the present study were limited to results spanning over the past 25-35 years.

Stress and Health

Stress is an important element in adaptation, placing demands on internal and/or external environmental challenges upon the individual (Tunk & Bellisimo, 1990). Stress is also denoted as the effect of the challenge upon the individual where the interaction between the individual and the environment come together. According to Baum, Gatchell, & Krantz (1997), stress increases the body's readiness and general state of activity and this arousal is linked with cognitive variables to our experiences of emotions. In stressful situations involving parental divorce, boys may experience severe shame, painful feeling so loss, and loneliness, while society places him in a gender straight jacket restricting his expression of emotions. Due to the stereotypes placed upon males by society, many of the feelings experienced may include sadness, vulnerability, helplessness, despair, and loss. All of these emotional symptoms are held inside the boy and create a pressure cooker effect. When the stress and pressure inside of him becomes overwhelming, he releases his emotions in a negative manner of acting out behaviors. These behaviors may include, but are not limited to, non-cooperative and disrespectful behavior (e.g. fighting, talking back, arguing, and hitting things and/or people). These situations occur because the boy knows he cannot express his feelings of shame or torment. Societal norms instilled in him, have created a fear of being considered weak and vulnerable. The expectations placed upon males by societal rules and norms include limited expression of emotions (e.g. fear, crying, and hugging, etc.). Fear or crying may lead to the idea that if males engage in these behaviors they are not considered to be a "real man". Real men are to be tough, never cry, fear nothing, and project a macho image.

The pressure from the family and society may lead to the acting out behaviors of a boy, and is a strong indicator that he is experiencing severe problems and pain, which needs to be addressed in a more appropriate and positive manner. This may include talking with parents, teachers, school counselors, or by seeking professional help. All of these areas of a boy's life are potential scenarios in which the boy's ability to cope with the situation and the utilization of effective coping skills may be demonstrated.

Theories of Coping and Intervention Skills

In addressing stress related to the effects of divorce on boys and the relationship with their mothers, emphasis needs to be given to modern methodologies. These theories include Selye's (1976) General Adaptation Theory of Stress, Seligman's (1992) Explanatory Styles of Coping, Forman's (1993) Coping Skills Interventions, and Hetherington and Blechman's (1996) Stress, Coping, and Resiliency related to the diathesis-stress model.

Selye's General Adaptation Theory of Stress

According to Baum, Gatchell, and Krantz (1997), Selye's theory is described in a three-stage response model or general adaptation syndrome (GAS). In the first stage, the "alarm reaction" or normal responses occur, as the organism becomes award of the presence of stressor(s) or stimulation. After the initial phase of lowered resistance, the system goes into counter shock and the body releases adrenocorticotrophic hormone (ACTH) into the blood stream, which stimulates the adrenal cortex (Rosenhan & Seligman, 1984).

According to Selye (1976), stressors are defined as causative agents and stress is the resulting condition or nonspecific response of the body to any demand. This process begins the direct effect of the stress upon the body, with the adrenal activity, increased cardiovascular and respiratory functions, and the release of glucocorticoids preparing the body for the "fight or flight" response. When the first stage is successful, the balance of the body is restored. The second stage, which is labeled the "stage of resistance", involves the internal responses, which stimulate tissue defense of help to destroy damaging substances (Selye, 1976). This process incorporates various coping mechanisms for adaptation and constant resistance to stressor(s), but there is a decrease in resistance to other types of stimuli (Baum, Gatchell, & Krantz, 1997).

During the second stage of resistance, coping mechanisms are applied for achievement of acceptable adaptation. Should occurrences be repeated constantly or prolonged in this stage, the organism is at a much greater risk for irreversible physiological damage (Baum, Gatchell, & Krantz, 1997). Selye's third stage, exhaustion, is considered to the result of the first two stages when the resistance does not terminate the stressor(s). During this stage internal responses continue, which cause tissue damage by inhibiting unnecessary or excessive defenses (Selye, 1976). This process causes depleted adaptive reserves by exhausting the coping mechanisms by long-term or repeated conflict with the stressor(s). Adaptive responses cease. These "diseases of adaptation" create illness, and in some cases death becomes inevitable (Baum, Gatchell, Krantz, 1997).

The resistance phase is the constant disruption of the body's homeostasis leading to the ineffective functions of the body's immune system. When the immune system no longer has the ability to fight back against stress or pathogens, the body becomes more vulnerable to stress related illnesses and disease. In order for the organism to maintain homeostasis, a proper balance is needed between the three stages of resistance and adaptation.

There are numerous diseases which impact children yearly. When the decrease in the immune system occurs according to Selye's GAS Theory, adding stress only places these children at greater risk for disease. The following types of diseases are linked to stress in children and adolescents: streptococcal infections (Meyer & Haggerty, 1962), rheumatoid arthritis, appendicitis, hemorrhaging in hemophiliacs (Heisel, Ream, Taitz, Rappaport, & Coddington, 1973), recurrent abdominal pain, chest pain, and headaches (Greene, Walker, Hickson, & Thompson, 1985; Hodge, Kline, Barrero, & Flannery, 1984; Pantell & Goodman, 1983), juvenile onset of diabetes

(Leaverton, White, McCormick, Smith, & Sheikholislam, 1980; Stein & Charles, 1971), asthma (Bedell, Giordani, Amour, Tavormina, & Boll, 1977), cystic fibrosis (Patterson & McCubbin, 1983; Smith, Gad, & O'Grady, 1983), and accidental injuries (Beaurtrias, Fergusson, & Shannon, 1982; Coddington & Troxell, 1980; Pailla, Rohsenow, & Bergman, 1976),

Rodriguez and Arnold (1998) found that children have a 50% greater risk factor of contracting asthma in the 12months following parental divorce. Research indicates that following divorce, a link between children's health and the experience of stress may lead to several of these health problems. Besides physical health issues being strongly related to stress and coping skills, there are psychological health and behavioral problems to be considered (Capaldi & Peterson, 1991; Cherlin, Furstenberg, chase-Lansdale, Kierman et al., 1991; Hetherington et al., 1998; Martinez & Forgatch, 2002). These problems include anxiety, depression, poor self-esteem, external locus of control (Barrearaz, 1981; Johnson, 1986; Lawrence & Russ, 1985), substance abuse (Wills, 1986), anorexia nervosa (Strober, 1984), suicidal behavior (Cohen-Sadler, Berman, & King, 1982), and poor school performance for all grade levels. All of these events have been correlated with doctors' visits, diagnosed illnesses, self- reported physical health problems, and missed days of school related to the illness (Gad & Johnson, 1980; Forman, 1993; Johnson & McCutheon, 1980). Boys especially will use many of these ailments to avoid going to school or participate in routine activities.

Research in the area of stress and coping has led to acting out and antisocial behaviors in boys due to stressful life experiences related to family circumstances (Capaldi & Peterson, 1991; Martinez, Jr. & Forgatch, 2002; Sun, 2001). Many of these boys have demonstrated negative behaviors before the parental divorce. In examining these factors some boys exhibit signs of psychopathology, while few survive becoming competent, well-functioning individuals. According to Hetherington & Blechman (1996), most researchers have concluded that there is no single pathway associated with the development of psychopathology. Consequently, different experiences will place boys at risk depending on the characteristics of the individuals and the larger context, in which they live and grow (Bronfenbrenner, 1986; Masten, Best, & Garmexy, 1990; Rutter, 1990; Sameroff & Seifer, 1990). Once sibling may be able to adapt and cope positively under stressful family circumstances, while another sibling is unable to overcome those same stressful events. Stress and coping is individual and no two people experience the same emotions and feelings when faced with trauma.

It is important to understand that 8-12 year old boys, who deal with stress from post-divorce, are expected to react differently from the ways in which girls react to stress. Stress has an effect on students' adjustment at school along with the lack of parental involvement from a single-parent home (Sun, 2001). Stress may lead to anxiety, depression, and a sense of loss of control. These factors impact students' academic success. Some of the early signs may include decreased confidence through not following rules, less attention to tasks or social skills, and a negative reaction to stress. Boys have been found to respond with aggression to stress (Rice, 2001). The aggression is most likely to be labeled or reported as maladjustment or behavioral problems, especially by teachers (Goodman, Brumley, Schwartz, & Purcell, 1993).

The foundation has been established for how boys externalize their problems and display antisocial behaviors following divorce. In a research study done by Cicchetti and Toth in 1996, boys' adaptation was linked to psychological and biological domains of development, which include both internal and external factors. Early patterns of attachment, responsiveness, and organization have been correlated to secure patterns of relatedness to the mothers. The positive patterns of relatedness to the mothers led the boys to have a more positive adaption, especially in connection with school functioning, ego resilience, and better test performance with less attendance problems, suspensions, and failure.

According to Martinez, Jr. and Forgatch (2002), variables such a negative parenting skills, antisocial mothers, and discipline impacted boys' stress and further enhanced behavioral problems and antisocial behaviors. Research findings indicate that sons are somewhat less close to both parents once the parents' divorce (Booth & Amato, 1994; Cooney, 1994). Boys that are exposed to more positive relationships with their mothers and their living environment will be able to demonstrate more positive behaviors of adaptation, coping skills, and adjustment within their lives (Capaldi & Patterson, 1991). These different types of behaviors stem from internal and external environmental factors and the boys' explanatory style.

Seligman's Explanatory Style

Another important factor surrounding everyday life, stressful events, and coping skills are the individual's explanatory style, which begins to develop during infancy. The explanatory style stems directly from one's place in the world e.g. valuable, worthless, deserving, helpless, or hopeless (Seligman, 1992). The explanatory style is either fundamentally optimistic or pessimistic thinking, which becomes an "entrenched habit of thinking" during childhood and adolescence and continues throughout the lifespan.

According to Seligman (1992), there are three crucial dimensions to explanatory style: permanence, pervasiveness, and personalization. The first phase is permanence, which deals with the length of time a negative event is perceived to last until the person decides to give up. The perception of the negative event being permanent produces long lasting pessimistic explanations. When negative events are seen as temporary, this is an optimistic explanation, which produces resilience.

The second phase, pervasiveness is related to the amount of time and is universal or specific. The universal approach produces pessimism across many situations making it a more stable approach (e.g. all teachers are unfair). The specific global approach produces optimism and it remains in the specific area of difficulty (e.g. Mr. Jones is unfair). The specific approach is much like compartmentalizing, one area is difficult, but is placed in a box and set aside so the person can go on with other aspects of their life. The universal approach can be illustrated like fabric, such as when the one thread breaks the whole fabric unravels (Seligman, 1992). The third phase, personalization is internal or external. The pessimistic approach occurs internally, when something negative happens, the individual blames oneself, and feels guilty and responsible. The optimistic approach is more external and the individual can blame the circumstances of the situation as being a one-time occurrence. In the pessimistic approach an individual may experience low self-esteem and believe oneself to be worthless, unlovable, and without self-respect.

In optimistic approach the individual blames external events and does not experience the loss of self-esteem. The individual has a more optimistic way to deal with the event. According to Seligman a person's explanatory style influences the way other people perceive one as an individual. It influences the person's physical and mental health (Seligman, 1992). A person's explanatory style leads to the habitual way of explaining and coping with traumatic events throughout one's lifespan.

Peterson, Vaillant, and Seligman (1988) published the results from a 35 year longitudinal study done on pessimistic explanatory style as a risk factor for physical illness. The results strongly indicated that pessimism was a risk factor for physical illness. Physical illness impacts the state of mental health as well.

Seligman and his colleagues have done numerous studies in assessing explanatory style by using the Attributional Style Questionnaire (ASQ). Burns and Seligman (1989) investigated the explanatory style across the life span and they found evidence of stability over 52 years. The results had similar findings to the results in 1988. The explanatory style for negative events may persist across the life span as internal, stable, and global, constituting an enduring risk factors for depression, low achievement, and physical illness (Burns & Seligman, 1989). A later study by Schulman, Castellon, and Seligman (1989) found that persons with a pessimistic explanatory style construe the causes of bad events as internal, stable, and global being more susceptible to helplessness, depression, and decreased immune functioning (Schulman, Castellon, & Seligman, 1989). The explanatory style of an individual is a major influence upon one's physical and mental health, coping skills, and the general ability to cope.

In Seligman's explanatory style there are three important factors that impact the child. First, is what the child learns from birth onward from the mother and father optimistically (positive) or pessimistically (negative) on a daily basis or routinely. This is the first impact toward a child learning an explanatory style, much like that of bonding and attachment. Second, is the form of criticisms the child hears from all significant adult figures as they mature. The feedback received from these significant others continues to form the child's explanatory style both optimistically, positive, and supportive feedback versus pessimistically, negative, and judgmental when the child fails. These comments, when the child makes an error may create emotional devastation of early losses and traumas, which impacts the child's disposition to be pessimistic or optimistic.

Third, the first reality of early loss and / or trauma impacts the child's explanatory style (e.g. loss of a parent through death, divorce, or separation). Children and adolescents taught optimist personal and social coping skills have an increased chance at more positive outcomes in life. An example of how a child experiencing the divorce of the parents, which is associate with both trauma and loss. My parents are getting divorced and this is my fault. The child would experience this as a stable persistent situation that is not going to change, which is going to impact their life and last forever. This could lead the child to feeling helpless, hopeless, and it could possible lead to depression.

According to Baum, Gatchel and Krantz (1997), optimism, pessimism, and one's prevailing worldview are important determinants of stress and its impact. At risk boys include those experiencing parental divorce, behavioral, and academic problems often times leading to psychopathology in adulthood. Research findings by Henderson, Hetherington, and Mekos (1996) found that each child differs in psychopathology even as siblings. The difference is partially explained because of the differential treatment given by the parents(s). Children, especially boys receiving higher levels of negativity from parents suffer greater psychopathology than do their siblings who experience less parental negativity. Boys can be taught these fundamental positive notions by what they hear and see demonstrated by parents, teachers, counselors, siblings, and professionals.

According to Froman (1993), coping can be viewed as a set of cognitive responses and behavioral responses used to deal with problematic events (Lazarus & Launier, 1978) in order to avoid being harmed by life strains (Pearlin & Schooler, 1978). Simplified coping is a set of useful individual reactions to stress that resolve, reduce, or replace a negative stressful state. There are specific reactions, which fall into six dimensions.

These are health and energy, positive beliefs, problem solving skills, social skills, social supports, and material resources.

There are three main areas of focus in assessing boys and adolescents for coping (Forman, 1993). First, there is the boy's social context for understanding their resources, styles, and efforts. Second, there is the boy's sensitivity to the environment and personal factors (e.g. temperament, emotional state, and attitude). Third, there is the boy's level of cognitive and social development. These three factors will indicate and influence how well the boy will cope with stressful experiences.

In the view of Folkman and Lazarus (1980), there are two major types of coping efforts, problem-focused and emotional-focused. Problem-focused efforts are used to alter or resolve the stress. Emotional-focused efforts are used to regulate the emotional response to a problem (e.g. cognitive reframing, selective attention, and relaxation). These factors, along with proven protective factors, such a temperamental characteristics of the child the family milieu, and external sources of support, feelings of self-esteem, and self-efficacy, all impact a child's resiliency.

Rutter (1987) suggested that children who encounter stressful situations and are able to successfully negotiate their way through these events, become more stress-resistant. They are more likely to seek out opportunities for growth in the future. Hetherington & Blechman (1996) suggested that what is basic to a number of risk and resiliency factors involves the capacity of the child to manage attention. These factors include attentional processes, which mediate between risk and psychopathology in children (Hetherington & Blechman, 1996).

Cognitive psychologists suggest that there are two separate attentional processes, the automatic processes involved in parallel processing of information, when many things are processed at the same time, and the attention demanding processes, which involve serial processing, where only one thing is processed at a time. Eysenck (1982) suggests a relationship between emotional arousal and performance. He states that changes may occur related to attentional selectivity, capacity, and the negative effects of distractibility. Selectivity may be an active coping response initiated to focus attention on a primary task. However, high levels of emotional arousal may decrease the ability to use parallel or shared processing (Hetherington & Blechman, 1996). The susceptibility to distractions originates with both internal and external events and decreased attention.

In the view of Hetherington & Blechman (1996) the processing of one's own emotional state with respect to organizing oneself for action towards some external goal needs conscious focus of attention. The executive function of emotion regulation requires the conscious focusing of attention away from the emotion-arousing event. These executive functions of attention require a dual ability with respect to the child's physiology. Furthermore it is suggested that these executive functions of attention are most importance in the child's resiliency stressful life events and are strongly influenced by the family (Hetherington & Blechman, 1996).

As explained by Forgatch et al. (1988), the effect of stress on boy's adjustment seemed to be both indirect and direct with a significant covariation between stress and adjustment. An analysis was conducted with significant findings, which provided support for the hypothesis that boy's adjustment problems would predict later levels of stress for both mother and son. This was found to last until 4 years later even after the levels of stress were partially relieved.

Coping skills represent a system of active information intertwined with learned physiological, social, cognitive, and/or effective behaviors used by the individual purposely to deal with stress or decrease a negative state (Forman, 1998). These coping skills interventions can be taught to boys and adolescents to improve their ability to deal with stressors in their daily lives in a positive constructive manner while decreasing the possibility of disease and adjustment problems. Useful coping skills include: relaxation techniques, social problem solving, improved social interactions, assertiveness training, self-instruction techniques, decrease irrational beliefs, stress reducing thought patterns, changing beliefs about failure and success, optimistic thinking and language, and self-control behaviors.

All of these skills enhance adolescent boys' abilities in coping with major and minor stressful situations encountered in everyday living, while increasing and strengthening their resiliency. These same skills would be useful for a boy within the age group of 8-12, in coping with parental divorce for two reasons. First, divorce is problematic with stressors that impede the boy's development [e.g. numerous life changes, social changes, and inter-parental conflict.] Second, divorce negates the boy's abilities to utilize parental resources (e.g. loss of contact with non-custodial parent (similar to death), loss of financial resources, and decrease in quality time with both parents). Since divorce, death, and single-parent families are a large part of the society we live in, coping skills should be a part of every child's (especially boys') education.

By educating the population to utilize effective coping skills, this would decrease many of the problems experienced by boys, thus increase their ability to communicate better, especially with their custodial mother. Effective coping skills and the ability to deal with stress in a positive manner will better assist young boys in life, while deterring the many adjustment problems brought on by outside factors e.g. divorce. Effective coping is relate dot the stages of the developmental process.

Erikson's Psychosocial Stages of Development

Erik Erikson (1902-1994) is noted for his psychosocial theory of development. Erikson disagreed with Freud on many points. One major point of difference was Freud placed too much emphasis on the sexual basis for behavior (Rice, 2001; Lefrancois, 1990). Erikson developed a theory in which he believed psychosocial motivations are needed as the driving force in human development and behavior. He believed humans have the ability to resolve their difficulties and conflicts as they are faced with them. Erikson set up eight stages of human development with a psychosocial task to be mastered during each stage.

Erikson also believed that the confrontation of each task produces a conflict with two possible outcomes. If the task was mastered a positive outcome would emerge and become incorporated into the personality creating a healthy ego with further development. Resolution of the stage developed a sense of personal competence within the individual (Lefrancois, 1990). However, if the task was not mastered and the conflict was unsatisfactorily resolved, the ego of the individual in question becomes damaged because of the unresolved outcome.

Erikson's theory is a useful positive way in which to look at human development. However, he did not take into account a person's constant and changing life. In today's society we need to still utilize Erikson's theory, but we need to take into account that we do not just go through a stage and resolve it in a permanent manner. People in today's society may very well revisit and confront many of Erikson's stages of development on multiple occasions throughout life. Fluctuation between these stages is understandable with the constant and continuous changes experienced in today's society. For example, a 50 year old woman finds her husband cheating on her, she would have completed the trust/mistrust issue between 0-1 year of age according to Erikson; however with the new dilemma in her life, trust will more than likely became an issue once again for her to confront. The three psychosocial stages to be addressed include the following: Trust verses Mistrust, Industry verses Inferiority, and Identity verses Identity Diffusion; and Marcia's Identity Diffusion.

Stage 1: Trust versus Mistrust

The stage of trust versus mistrust begins as an infant and lasts until approximately 1 year of age. Erikson stated, "By trust I mean an essential trustfulness of others as well as a fundamental sense of one's own trustworthiness" (Erikson,

1968). During this stage infants learn to trust their caregivers, parents, or significant others in their life for protection comfort, affection, and the basic needs to sustain life (e.g. food, clothing, shelter, safe environment, etc.). Not only do children learn to trust others, they are also learning to trust themselves.

Trust is one of the most basic components of a healthy personality (Erikson, 1959). The conflict infants are usually faced with during this stage relates to the conflict between mistrust of the world around and about them. They know little of the world of the inclination to develop a trusting attitude toward that world. The primary caregiver for this age group is usually the mother. The relationship the caregiver and the child experience together impacts the stage of the child's life and largely impacts the child's ability to resolve this stage conflict.

The relationship between the caregiver and child impacts the child's gradual realization that the world is predictable, safe, and loving. If the world is unpredictable and the caregiver rejecting, the infant will grow up to be mistrustful and anxious in relating to others. Breast feeding, bottle feeding, smiling, touching, direct eye contact, listening, speaking, tone, physical closeness, and laughter all begin the stage of trust/mistrust leading to a positive emotional attachment and bonding of infant/caregiver. "Parents who were closely attached to their parents in close, affectionate relationships are more likely to establish such relationships with their own children" (Rice, 2001; Fonagy, Steele, & Steele, 1991). Parent's own emotional experiences, expressive behaviors, and personality traits are significant predictors of the level of security of their infant-parent attachment, but these in turn, are partly the result of the kind of relationships their parents developed with them (Izad et al., 1991; Rice 2001). Children with a strong sense of safety and security may develop multiple close attachments, however this does not mean that the caregiver can be changed constantly. Attachment is a dialogue that goes on between the caregiver and the child in a stable, secure, loving environment. (Trust / attachment will be addressed later on).

Stage 4: Industry versus Inferiority

Erikson's fourth stage of the psychosocial developmental theory is industry versus inferiority, which occurs approximately during 6-12 years of age. This stage of development corresponds to Freud's latency period. During this stage children have an increasing need to interact with others and find acceptance by their peers. Children are learning to meet the needs of home life, school, and develop a sense of self-worth through their accomplishments and interactions with others. While in this stage children begin to accept the challenge of new opportunities to learn those things they think are important to their culture, and by doing so they hope to become someone or to be competent. Recognition and praise by parents, teachers, and peers are important to the development of a positive self-concept. The resolution of this stage depends upon the responses of significant others in the child's life. If the child meets with much negativity is always being demeaned with little praise or rarely regarded, the outcome may be a lasting sense of inferiority.

In addressing 8-12 year old boys relating to the stage of industry versus inferiority, a time period of mastery begins with the development of a sense of self-worth. The process of discovery is important to the boy's identity and independence. Peer acceptance and interaction becomes a vital part of the boy's life. Boys need the ability to accomplish tasks and feel a sense of competence, while learning those things important to their culture. The idea of becoming someone with something to offer to his society gives him a sense of industry. Parents, teachers, schools, society, and the boy's efforts are all factors in his successful resolution of this stage conflict (Lefrancois, 1990). Inferiority may prevail should the boy not resolve the conflict.

Inferiority may well develop from failure to successfully resolve prior stages of autonomy or initiative. Another explanation of inferiority in the current stage would be that the boy is receiving negative feedback about his work with little or no praise or reward. Family life may not prepared the boy for school life and how to do things. A boy's development of thinking and feeling he will never be good enough or smart enough may emerge becoming a dangerous influence throughout the remainder of his school years or a detriment to his future. Boys experiencing these particular feelings of inferiority may lead them to frustration, anger, and fits of rage. According to Erikson (1968), every child needs a feeling of competence, that is, "the free exercise of dexterity and intelligence in the completion of serious tasks....for this is the lasting basis for cooperative participation in productive adult life".

Boys experiencing the turmoil of parental post-divorce adjustment during the ages of 6-11 are at greater risk for high levels of stress and health issues in facing the conflict of industry versus inferiority. While struggling for personal identity, independence, peer and social acceptance, their need to feel competent and worthwhile may be drastically disrupted creating frustration and anger towards their parents, siblings, and the situation of divorce. During the ages of 8-11, these outbursts of anger or fits of rage will be directed towards the parents and siblings.

In situations of divorce, the custodial parent, which is usually the mother, may become the target of the anger, rage, and outbursts from the son. These acting out behaviors place a greater strain upon the mother and son relationship. These conflicts while creating greater adjustment problems for the boys also decrease their chances for positive resolution of the stage development conflict. Without successful resolutions of the stage conflict the boy will carry forth his negative feelings and frustrations into the next stage conflict of identity versus identity diffusion.

Stage 5: Identity versus Identity Diffusion

In the fifth stage of Erikson's psychosocial developmental theory, identity versus identity diffusion occurs with the emphasis placed upon the development of a strong sense of identity or ego. This stage is closely related to Freud's genital period. This particular stage is where boys around the age of 11 and older begin shedding childhood and enter adulthood. This time period is usually referred to as the adolescence period.

During this stage Erikson places emphasis on the ego as becoming more evident in the child's life. Development of a strong sense of self and a solid identity will help boys achieve a strong sense of identity. The conflict that occurs relates to the strong sense of the self and self-concepts. In adolescence we find young people torn between early acceptances of a clearly defined self and a variety of roles they could possibly become through the influence of peers and other factors. Erikson stated that it is no longer about discovering anymore who they are, but rather it is on the development of one of the many potential selves.

Boys, especially, need to have a progressive sense of continuity and inner wholeness of who he has been and what he anticipates in becoming in the future (Erikson, 1968). The fundamental aspect is the development of high self-esteem (self-worth). The boy must become a whole person in his own right with many rapid changes occurring in his life (e.g. physical growth, genital maturation, and social awareness).

The wholeness to which Erikson refers is the send of the inner identity. The sense of inner identify includes how the boy conceives himself and his perceptions of how others view him and what they expect from him. In this stage the crisis is the conflict between accepting, choosing, or discovering an identity that conforms to societal norms and to the boys own expectation. Marcia's research (1966) has given further clarity to the stage of identity by Erikson. Marcia describes the stage as a time when adolescents achieve a positive stable identity or identity status.

Marcia's Identity Diffusion

According to Marcia (1966), ego identity and identity diffusion refer to the polar outcomes of the psychosocial crisis occurring in late adolescence. This was found to be a time of growing occupational and ideological commitment. The individual is facing taking on adult roles of getting a job, becoming an adult, and becoming a citizen. The individual is trying to synthesize childhood identification in such a manner that he or she can both establish a relationship with the society at large and maintain a feeling of continuity within him or herself.

It is important to note that this is a time period where choices are constant with ongoing struggles. This ego identity status consists of crisis and commitment in regard to occupational choice, religion, and political ideology. Crisis refers to the adolescent's period of engagement in choosing among meaningful alternatives. Commitment refers to the degree of personal investment the individual exhibits. Several studies have concluded those individuals that who have achieved ego identity appear to be less confused in self-definition and experience less anxiety (Marcia, 1966).

As explained by Lefrancois (1990), individuals who have not developed a mature sense of identity by late adolescence may become labeled as playboys, disturbed, or as fun seekers. These individuals have low self-esteem, high anxiety, enjoy being isolated, demonstrate a lack of self-confidence, and a decreased sense of moral reasoning.

Boys experiencing conflict during the stage of identity while dealing with parental post- divorce issues may have enhanced period of confusion followed by time periods of rebellion. The rebellion comes about from the stress of the situation from parents, peers, and the environment. According to Erikson (1980), when a child feels or perceives his environment is trying to radically deprive him of all forms of personal expressions, which permit him to develop and to integrate into the next step in his ego identity. Then he will resist with the astounding strength encountered in animals that are suddenly forced to defend their lives. These instinctual urges may be so powerful and strong, in fact, that they will influence the boy to make poor choices, even when the boy feels their reaction is needed for survival.

In following these choices, boys will not achieve a positive sense of personal identity which may lead to problems of sexuality, relationship problems in making commitments, a lack of independence, increased aggressive behaviors, and disturbance disorder. These types of behaviors increase the strain between the mother and son relationship, especially when separation or divorce occurs within the family unit. Failure relating to major tasks of development results in cumulative risk for future maladaptation and psychopathology (Luther, Burack, Cincchetti, & Weisz, 1997).

Specific types of maladaptive behaviors and psychopathology may lead to drug use and abuse, criminal behaviors, alcohol and tobacco use, suicide, deviant behaviors, and risky sexual activity. Much of these behaviors may well relate back to the developmental processes over short or long periods of time and to how the boy attached or bonded to mother, father, or caregiver figures as an infant.

Importance and theories of Attachment and Bonding

Attachment and Bonding

The emotional development of children is concerned with the development of their feelings and expressions in relation to their parents, peers, other people, and literally everything in their world (Rice, 2001). Emotions are powerful motivators in behavior, communication, pleasure and pain, and a role in moral development. The most important are those emotional bonds of attachment made with those persons in our lives through intimate connections (e.g. parents, caregivers, or a spouse/significant other). In addressing attachment and bonding, a variety of theories have been offered.

These theories include psychoanalytic, psychosocial, learning, ethological, and ecological. Each position makes specific assumptions about the role of attachment in the infant development, the variables important for attachment to develop, and the processes underlying the development of attachment (Hetherington & Parke, 1979).

Psychoanalytic Theory

Erik Erikson (1963, 1968) suggested that the cornerstone of a vital personality is formed during infancy as the child interacts with the parents of caregivers. These relationships from birth begin to develop a sense of trust and security relating to Erikson's stage of psychosocial development, trust versus mistrust. Infants learn basic trust as they can depend on the caregiver that meets their needs and provides them with protection, comfort, and affection. When these needs are not met infants then becomes very mistrustful and insecure.

Margaret Mahler, a clinical psychologist, emphasizes the importance of the mother-child relationship (Mahler, Pine, & Bergman, 1975; Rice, 2001). Infants from birth to 2 months go through an autistic phase with their only awareness of the mother as the agent that meets their basic needs (Rice, 2001). From approximately 2-5 months infants enter a second phase, symbiosis where they establish dependency on the mother. In this stage a solid foundation is constructed which serves as a basis for growth and independence. Mahler believed a sensitive and responsive mother would encourage a symbiotic relationship with the infant. A less sensitive mother may create frustration in the infant causing the infant to fuse with her creating insecurity (Rice, 2001).

Learning Theory

Learning theory like the psychoanalytic theorists have stressed the importance of the feeding situation for the development of attachment (Hetherington & Parke, 1979; Sear, Maccoby, & Levin, 1957). The caregiver/mother acquires a positive value through association with the satisfaction and reduction in hunger, a primary drive. The caregiver/mother, as a result of being paired with the drive reducing activity of the feeding, acquires a secondary reinforcement property and consequently is valued in her own right. This leads to the presence of the caregiver/ mother as becoming satisfying. The child develops an acquired need for contact with the caregiver/ mother, which is referred to as attachment (Hetherington &

Parke, 1979). The feeding situation has been challenged and criticized by several.

In 1959, Harlow and Zimmerman conducted a study in which it was found that hunger reduction does not necessitate attachment development. According to Hetherington and Parke (1979), the important feature of the learning theory explanation is that attachment is not an innate or instinctual process, but rather it develops over time as a result of satisfying interaction with key people in the child's environment. Learning theorists view attachment as a two way process, moreover-where the infant and the caregiver/mother develop attachments to each other gradually-that is, over the first 6-7 months of the child's life.

Social Learning Theory

Albert Bandura's (1977, 1982), social learning theory has a major influence on the conceptualization of how models play a crucial role in the acquisition of behavior. Children learn behaviors from observing their parents and significant role models. Then the behaviors are repeated from the child. In attachment and bonding children utilize skills learned from these important caregivers and in later life display similar behaviors with their own children.

There are three main points of the social learning theory. First, there is the emphasis placed upon new behaviors, which can be learned without direct reinforcement, learning by observing how others behave and how they are treated. Second, the importance of what children think and how they react is impacted by the responses of others thoughts and actions. The child is viewed as an active force in their development, not a "tablua rasa"- that is, a blank slate upon which experience is written. Third, mental representations of actions can be developed upon observation, encoded, and then be performed at a later time.

Ethological Theory

John Bowlby's ethological theory (1958, 1969, 1973), places emphasis upon the reciprocal nature of the attachment process. Bowlby has suggested that attachment is a result of a set of instinctual responses, which are important for the protection and survival of the species (Hetherington & Parke, 1979). The mother is biologically prepared to respond to the infant and the infant is predisposed to respond to the sights, sounds, and nurturance provided by the mother.

Examples of infant behaviors include crying, smiling, sucking, clinging, and following; all of these elicit, a necessary response from the mother to protect the infant, which promotes contact between the mother and child. According to Hetherington and Parke (1979), the value of the ethological theory is the emphasis that is placed upon the active role of the infant's early social signaling system as well as the prominence of mutual attachment.

Ecological Theory

Bronfenbrenner's ecological approach (1979), emphasizes that development is influenced by a variety of factors in the individual's immediate and more distal environment and that it is important to examine the interrelationship among these factors instead of attempting to identify individual factors or causes (Luthar, Burack, Cicchetti, & Weisz, 1997). Brofenbrenner (1979) believed that the multivariate-interactional approach represents the true nature of human behavior more accurately, while using a more useful heuristic device for greater explanatory power in the describing and predicting human development.

Brofenbrenner's (1979) theory has three defining characteristics. He explains that the individual is first perceived as an active growing organism who moves into and restructures the environment in which it (he) lives. Second, environments constantly act upon and adjust themselves to each other and this factor needs to be recognized by the scholarly community. Third, there is the need to study the individual's behavior in a variety of settings, paying special attention to interconnections among the factors and consider the impact upon development (Brofenbrenner, 1979).

In summary all of the theories and theorists have made a contribution towards the connection of attachment theory of the infant and caregiver/mother. "Attachment theorists believe that children's bonding with their parents (the working models) is revised and adjusted on the basis of children's continuing interactions with them (Bowlby, 1982; Bretherton & Walters, 1990; Crittenden, 1990; Lamb, 1981; Lamb, Thompson, Garner, & Charnov, 1985). Sun (2001) found children are molded by their parents' behavior of exhibiting fear, anger, and aggression.

Infants not only develop attachments to their mothers, but to a variety of other persons including their fathers. In the changing world of today's society and the changing of cultural views, fathers often take a much more active role in early infancy, which increases the chances that they will develop, a strong attachment to the infant. Fathers serve as an attachment figure for their offspring and today play an important role in the infant's life as well as the mother (Hetherington & Parke, 1979).

According to Schaffer and Emerson (1964), a Scottish study found that infants were attached to adults who responded quickly to their demands and cries by spontaneously reacted and initiated interactions with the child. Children receiving a combination of attention and stimulation from fathers and having received only physical care from the mothers; were found to have parental attachment to the fathers, despite the contact with the mothers. The findings from other longitudinal studies done by Ainsworth (1973), Ainsworth & Bell, (1969), and Caldwell, Wright, Honig, & Tannenbaum (1970) indicate that parental behavior and stimulation in response to the infant's signals are important in attachment formation.

In view of Luther, Burack, Cicchetti, & Weisz (1997), repeated abusive or neglectful parents increase the chances for abused children to become mistrustful and predisposed the victims to form insecure attachment relationships. Findings indicate abusive mothers are more hostile and intrusive than non-abusive mothers form similar socioeconomic backgrounds (Crittenden, 1981; Lyons-Ruth, Connell, & Zoll, 1989). Abused infants are often insecurely attached to their abusive parents-either one or both, it should be noted (Carlson, Cicchetti, Barnett, & Braunwald, 1989; Crittenden, 1988; Lambe, Gaensbauer, Malkin, & Schultz, 1985).

Abused children often protect themselves from the effects of inconsistent parenting by processing information about intimate relationships in ways that minimize their feelings of rejection. This process results in the formation of inaccurate representations of their parents. These defense mechanisms help children cope in the short term, but may foster distorted interpersonal relationships and create a larger context of problems later on in the child's life. Studies have found children who have insecure attachment relationships as infants and toddlers have a more difficult time developing and maintaining healthy peer relationships later on in life (Sroufe, 1983).

As infants grow into adolescence, both individual and family attachment models must be reconsidered and reorganized, for these theories are based on models that are rapidly changing, much like that of the adolescent life (Main et al., 1985; Ricks, 1985; Sroufe & Fleeson, 1986). The stress of impending separation and growing autonomy may bring about issues and patterns of interactions from earlier attachment relationships. There are numerous studies that suggest attachment and insecurity may be relate to problematic behaviors and deviance. Attachment organizations possibly are the link between the interaction of other aspects of development that led to or away from problematic behaviors (Allen, Moore, & Kuperminc, 1997).

The security in attachment organizations, refers to the infant's secure categorization or in the adolescent's / adult's categorization as "autonomous yet valuing of attachment," which is to be considered the optimal outcome of the attachment process (Ainsworth, Blehar, Waters, & Wall, 1978;

Bowlby, 1980; Main et al., 1985). In adolescence/adulthood, this security is internalized and characterized by the ability of one to think and speak about attachment relationships in a logical, internally consistent, and balance manner (Main & Goldwyn, in press).

Children with secure attachment relationships enter into adolescence, where there are still autonomy issues. These issues may lead to predictable family conflicts with the family unit (Allen, Moore, & Kupermine, 1997). However, in childhood studies there is a link between attachment security and fewer problems with compliance and autonomy struggles relating to parents (Ainsworth et al., 1978; Alexander, Waldron, Barton, & Mas, 1989; Allen, Moore, & Kuperminc, 1979; Lay, Waters, & Park, 1989; Russo, Cataldo, & Cushing, 1981; Sroufe et al., 1984; Waters, Wippman, & Sroufe, 1979).

When this occurs within the nuclear family of a secure strong dyad, the relationship is characterized by strong efforts by all parties to maintain connections between parents and child. Kobak, et al., (1993), has referred to the importance in adolescence as the "goal corrected partnership" in which both parents and adolescents adjust their behaviors in line with the other's communicated needs and desires as both seek a common goal of fostering adaptive adolescent development (Kobak, Cole, Ferenz-Gilles, & Fleming, 1993).

Studies have found that better communication patterns exist in families of secure adolescents, with parents knowing more about what their adolescent thinks, being trusted and confided in more, and there are lower levels of conflict as characterized by multilateral versus unilateral decision making (Allen & Bell, 1995). Parents' and teens' attachment systems may become taxed repeatedly as the adolescent explores values, behaviors, and ultimately residences that are not shared with their parents. These explorations may bring about change in stability or the nature of the relationship between the adolescent and parent.

However, these explanations are less likely to have a major impact when the relationship between the child and parents is fundamentally secure and intact with the parents remaining psychologically available to the child (Allen, Moore, & Kuperminc, 1979). When secure attachments to both parents exist, the child will develop a positive self-image, a sturdy self-esteem that allows them genuinely to love themselves. By possessing a love for themselves, they will have the ability to be free to love others in a more genuine manner (Erikson, 1998).

In insecure attachment organizations there are three basic patterns that have been categorized: (a) dismissing/ avoidant; (b) preoccupied/ ambivalent; (c) unresolved or disorganized attachment with respect to past loss or trauma/ disorganized (Ainworth et al., 1978; Main & Goldwyn, in press; Main & Solomon, 1986). Each of these insecure attachment organizations reflects at least some degree of functional deficit in thinning about, discussing, and evaluating attachment experiences (Main & Goldwyn, in press). Specific manifestations of different types of insecure attachment organizations, particularly as they relate to problematic behaviors can be expected to differ somewhat across classifications.

The unresolved / disorganized attachment organization typically applies when an attachment figure dies, there is a loss, or the specific person behaves in a frightening or abusive manner. This status is linked to aggressive and hostile child behavior and to serious adolescent psychopathology (Allen, Hauser, & Borman-Spurrell, 1996; Lyons-Ruth, Alpern, & Repacholi, 1993). Increased family conflict around other issues during attachment organization (Allen, Moore, & Kuperminc, 1979).

Relating these theories to boys' ages 8-12 years of age, there are many factors that may well take effect and impact the relationship between the mother and son following a divorce. There is the possible lack of attachment established between the mother and the soon during infancy. The loss of attachment with the father figure following a divorce may be demonstrated by angry behavior in the boy, which may lead to more aggressive behaviors toward the mother because they boy may blame the mother for the loss of the father. Once these relationships become taxed with increased stress, the psychosocial stages of development may become interrupted causing increased confusion.

These external and internal problems for adolescent boys may become even more problematic due to unspoken counter-productive gender roles. Boys learn the restrictions of emotional expression related to mirroring parental restricted expression and social learning. These expressions of emotions can be particularly repressive because the expression of feelings is essential to the grieving and loss process. Emotional expressions are needed as well as for the bonding and security in relationships with others, (e.g. both with the immediate family and others). When boys from divorced families are forced into choosing sides and/or become confused about how to relate to their parents, they become a part of the family's fragile status quo. They may begin to explore outside their secure attachment organization.

The divorced situation may also lead boys to more severe problematic behaviors, deviance, and encounters with the law. Forced separation from either parent e.g. divorce, leaves emotional scars because separation assaults the essential connections needed with both parents (Erikson, 1998). However, separation is not just emotional. Separation can lead to physical and psychological scars as well. These scars create dysfunction for the child. When not handled in an appropriate manner separation creates more dysfunctions as these children of divorced families grow up and go forth to have families of their own. In the world today we can see the changes caused by separation and divorce within the shape and nature of families, economics, values, and belief systems, and within our society as a whole. This raises the question of why some individuals are more vulnerable with a greater risk of maladjustment, while others become stronger and more resilient, overcoming difficulties and leading functional lives.

Vulnerability, Risk, Resilience, and the
Diathesis-Stress Model

Vulnerability, resiliency, and risk are based on a model of human development that emphasizes the interactions between the individual's capabilities and the circumstances in which the individual lives (Sternberg, Lamb, & Dawud-Noursi, 1997). "Vulnerability, it should be explained, refers to a particular weakness, deficit, or defect of the individual.

Risk, on the other hand, pertains more to the interaction of the environment and the individual. Risk may also predispose the individual to a negative or undesirable outcome (Cowan, Cowan, & Schulz, 1996; Solnit, 1984).

Vulnerabilities increase the probability of negative outcomes in the presence of risk and these may include both internal (biological and psychological) and external (interfamilial and social-environmental) conditions that detract from the attainment of competence and successful adaption. Rutter (1990), states that risk and vulnerability are indicators of a complex matrix of processes and mechanisms that impact the individual's development. These two factors appear to operate through influences on competence or incompetence at progressive stages of the child's development. Thus it can be seen that the overall develoOpmetnal outcome is affected no only by the risk or vulnerability (its presence or absence), but through the interplay that occurs between the factors and prior levels of adaptation as well, according to the literature (Cicchetti & Toth, 1997; Cicchetti & Tucker, 1994; Sroufe, Englund, & Kreutzer, 1990; Zigler & Glick, 1986).

This approach implies that each individual has a unique constellation of resources and weaknesses that interact with the environmental challenges (Sternberg, Lamb, & Dawud-Noursi, 1997). This constellation of resources and weaknesses is uniquely personal. In addition, it is inclusive of the individual's biological, psychological, cognitive, emotional, developmental, environmental, and social factors. Hetherington and Blechman (1996) explaining that resilience, stress resistance, or invulnerability refers to processes that operate in the presence of risk to produce outcomes as good or better than those obtained in the absence of risk. Resilient individual are those who do not simply avoid the most negative outcomes associated with risk, but demonstrate adequate or more than adequate adaption in the face of adversity. Individuals, especially children are in no way impervious to stress or catastrophe. Resilience may be a better descriptive term for the idea that some individuals or families possess physiological strengths, psychological resourcefulness, and interpersonal skills that enable them to respond more successfully to major challenges and to grow from the experience.

Masten and Garmexy (1984) argued that active coping and stress can build or enhance resilience with repeated measures. Resilience can be enhanced by the mastery experiences that develop and refine new coping skills. Resilience can lead to positive and optimistic outcomes that occur in spite of or because of the individual's exposure to risk (Cowan, Cowan, & Schulz, 1997; Hetherington & Blechman, 1997). According to Hopf (2010) significant stressors associated with divorce, approximately 75-80 percent of children develop into well-adjusted adults with no lasting psychological or behavioral problems (Kelly & Emery, 2003), however there is still 20-25 percent of the children that have lasting effects. Hetherington and Blechman (1997) suggested the conception of resilience helps to determine priorities for preventative intervention in learning how to nurture and foster mechanisms that lead to coping when faced with ongoing and anticipated stressors and risk.

In addressing the issues of vulnerability, stress, risk, and resilience, the diathesis-stress model is a useful tool that addresses the interaction of vulnerability, stressful life events, and the possible outcomes. The model posits that the diathesis may be comprised of psychological factors (e.g. cognitive distortions, learned helplessness, explanatory style) or biological factors (e.g. genetic factors, neurotransmitter irregularities (hormonal from stress), or brain abnormalities. The environmental and social stressors (e.g. divorce, loss of parental figure or job) added to the diathesis increase the risk of developing an ineffective coping skills, a disorder, and/ or problematic behaviors.

Two important factors that need to be taken into account in using the diathesis-stress model are protective factors (e.g. explanatory style, coping skills, resources, and social support) and risk factors (e.g. defense mechanisms, marital conflict, parent's methods, gender, etc.). However, some of the protective factors may become both protective factors as well as risk factors, especially following the divorce of their parents.

Literature Conclusion

In reviewing the literature regarding the effects of divorce on boys' 8-12 years of age, it is strongly suggested that boys are more poorly adjusted following divorce. There are many factors that impact and fit into the diathesis-stress model, such as, the boy's age at the time of divorce, the first traumatic event in the boy's life. His psychosocial stage of development, loss of father, aggressive behavior, maternal stress, antisocial behavior, socioeconomic disadvantage, ineffective discipline, ineffective coping skills, poor monitoring of the boy, behavioral problems, explanatory style, and how and what type of attachment and bonding they have experienced with both parents, and etc.

Greene & Leslie (1989) researched post-divorce adjustment of boys be examining two aspects of the mother-son relationship; maternal support and coercion as reported by the sons. Further they examined the extent to which the mother's attitude toward the ex-husband might affect her interactions with her son and his level of aggressive. Findings suggested that there is a relationship between a mother's attitude toward of ex-husband and how supportive and coercive she is in her interactions with her son. The mother's explanatory style may well impact her attitude towards the ex-husband and her interactions with the son. These levels of support and coercion are proposed to be associated with the level of aggression a son displays. The mother's attitude toward her ex-husband was found to have a direct effects on how emotionally supportive and coercive her son perceived her to be two years following the divorce. A mother who was negative towards the father, for example, was seen as both less supportive and more coercive.

Empirical data supports the connection between a son's perception of his mother's attempts to coerce him and his level of aggression in school (Greene & Leslie, 1989). It is suggested that the more coercive a mother is thought to be, the more overt and passive aggressive the son will become. When this type of relationship is created between the mother and the son following the divorce of the parents, the son has greater adjustment problems. Other factors that need to be addressed are the father's role in the son's life and the father's attitude towards the mother, and the father's explanatory style.

The mother's social and economic context also plays a role in the mother-son relationship (Greene & Leslie, 1989). Mothers who are often struggling financially to reestablish family life, which is impacted by societal factors impinging upon the family. All of these factors as well impact the patterns of family interaction and development along with the adjustment and reactions of the so (Capaldi & Patterson, 1991; Clarke-Stewart, et al., 2000; Martinez, Jr., & Forgatch, 2002; Sun, 2001).

In another study conducted by Olweus (1980), the researcher found that four main interfamilial factors could explain a considerable amount of variance in the habitual level of aggression displayed in Swedish adolescent boys. These effects were found to be additive, which implies that the more negative childhood conditions a young boy is exposed to and the more active and hotheaded his temperament, the more likely he is to develop into an aggressive adolescent (Olweus, 1980).

The findings included that the mother's negativism and permissiveness for aggression had the greatest causal effects. The implication is that a young boy who gets too little love, too little interest from his mother, too much freedom, and lack of clear limits with regard to aggressive behavior has a greater chance at becoming an aggressive adolescent than one who has not experienced these conditions. In a longitudinal research study completed by Zill, Morrison, and Coiro (1993), findings suggested there were three factors that influence boys adjustment to divorce; gender, age, and remarriage. Boys from divorced families were found to be more likely to show consequences such as behavioral problems or an increase in high school drop-out rate. Boys' 12-16 years of age were found to more vulnerable to the effects of disruption, however, boys are generally more prone to these difficulties.

According to Boruin & Henggeler (1987), the boy's age at the time of the divorce impacts the degree of positive mother-son reciprocity during adolescence. Further, findings suggest that boys, 8-12 years of age using the concrete operational stage, have greater interpersonal reasoning skills. They are more able to emotionally align with the mother (Borduin & Henggeler, 1987). Zill, Morrison, and Coico (1993) found that girls were more likely to develop poor relationships with their mothers over boys.

Summary of Results and Chapter Conclusion

In conclusion, research has identified numerous variable that impact adjustment in boys' 8-12 years of age following divorce. However, the findings indicate there is no specific decline in the relationship between mother and son following divorce. According to Greene & Leslie (1989), most of all patent-child relationships, regardless of whether they are a single or two parent family, are characterized by some level of struggle or tension as the preadolescent child becomes increasingly egocentric and less cooperative in their dealings with parents.

Borduin & Henggeler (1987) further suggested that the task to raise an adolescent son is generally more difficult in divorced than intact families. However, the association between adolescent behavioral maladjustment and mother-son relationship is similar across all types of family structures with no empirical evidence provided that adolescent boys from divorced or intact families are any different to raise in today's society. Research studies strongly indicate adolescent girls internalize their feelings and behaviors, where adolescent boys will display more aggressive acting out behaviors following divorce of the parents.

Research studies are needed in the areas of the mother-son perspective relating to divorce effects, attachment and bonding, coping and defenses mechanism, risk, resiliency, and adjustment. The impact of family disruption and parent loss upon the psychosocial stages of development are impacted as boys are placed at a greater risk for adverse outcomes when parents' divorce. Another area to explore is the connection between an individual's explanatory style, coping, and defense mechanisms and the impact upon an individual's health and one's diathesis and stress leading to possible disorders and behavioral problems.

CHAPTER 3

CONCLUSIONS: AND USE OF DIATHESIS-STRESS MODEL

Introduction

Integrative Summary of the Literature

The Impact of Divorce on Boys

According to research reviews (Amato, 1993; Emery & O'Leary, 1982), children of divorce exhibit more acting-out behaviors (e.g. aggression, conflict with the caretaker/ parent, school authorities, etc.) as well as maladaptive and internally directed behaviors such as withdrawal, depression, and anxiety, just to mention a few. The literature has concluded that children exposed to occurrences of martial conflict may not be able to deal with such conflict and may react emotionally to the stress of the marital conflicts with feelings of distress, anxiety, and depression. There are numerous other repercussions, of course. For example, children of divorce are less likely to perform academically, have a lower academic self-concept, and are less motivated to achieve. These adjustment difficulties are sometimes directly divorce-related, and sometimes due more to problems in the parents functioning after the divorce (Hetherington & Blechman, 1996).

Sun (2001) concluded from his research study that boys were more aggressive, impulsive, and anxious in unpredictable situations following parental divorce. He also concluded that boys showed increased signs of maladjustment and behavioral problems. Cherlin et al. (1991) found that boys who experienced family dissolution between the ages of 7 and 11 years of age exhibited higher levels of behavioral and academic problems. Morrison and Cherlin (1995) found elevated behavioral problems among boys who had experienced post-parental divorce were associated with downward social mobility. In previous research studies (Hetherington et al., 1979; Howell et al., 1997; Jenkins & Smith, 1993; Mott et al., 1997; Simons, 1996; Wallerstein & Blakeslee, 1989; Wallerstein & Kelly, 1980; Zaslow, 1988), investigators found that boys were more adversely affected by parental divorce, particularly in the areas of social adjustment and the mother-son relationship (Amato & Keith, 1991). Clarke-Stewart et al. (2000) found that boys were impacted more intellectually, Martiznez and Forgatch (2002) found that boys in families that experience a series of disruptions in family structure were at a greater risk for adverse outcomes.

More current literature reviewed in this study has indicated that the effects of divorce on children may vary by gender, age, developmental level, and quality of noncustodial parenting (Goodman et al., 1993; Howell, Portes, & Brown, 1997; Simons et al., 1999; Sun, 2001). This research supported earlier findings by Ainsworth et al. (1978), Bordun and Henggeler (1987), and Zaslow (1988). However, it is important to again mention the age of the studies include in the present critical review-in fact, the bulk of the research-were conducted in the last 10-35 years. There needs to be more research in this area and boys as well as girls should be given equal consideration. For current investigative studies were identified by this researcher.

One study conducted by Martinez and Forgatch (2002) suggested that mothers who manage effective parenting through such stressful circumstances might be able to buffer the negative effects of adverse outcomes on their sons, however the mother's effectiveness would depend in depth upon her emotional stability, parenting practices, and explanatory style. Further impacts upon her parenting abilities would depend upon other relationships following the divorce, which she may have with other partners. These relationships could take away from her time and the effort she puts forth with her children, thus placing her at a greater risk for disrupted parenting practices.

Many factors influence the mother and son relationship. The son's attachment and bonding with the mother is a vital part of his life. The attachment and bonding between the mother and son becomes threatened in the post-divorce adjustment phase due to significant partnering relationships of the mother. The stage of development of the boy impacts the relationship with both of his parents during post-divorce adjustment. Other factors include the mother's socioeconomic status, educational level, mental health, and coping techniques, self-esteem, and parenting skills. Family transitions and stress have been found to decrease a family's coping abilities while increasing the vulnerability of negative behaviors and adjustment problems in both parents and children.

From the review, it was discovered that, while some studies (Kelly, 1993) find that boys have more adjustment problems that girls do, investigative research involving both genders found that boys do less well than girls only in terms of their social adjustment (Amato & Keith, 1991). More conflict was noted between mothers and sons. On the other hand, conflict levels between mothers and daughters increase during the adolescent developmental period in life. The review revealed divorce had adverse effects on children of all ages. However, it appeared there were no specific types of negative effects that could be attributed to any given age of the child or children. However, Wallerstein and Kelly (1980) conclude from their research on how children and parents cope with divorce that there may be age-related divorce concerns that are linked to children's levels of cognitive and emotional development. Preschoolers were more likely to focus on maintaining emotional security and relationships with both parents; they also need more regulated activities and routine in their home as well as their school environments. (Wallerstein and Kelly, 1980) explained that during middle childhood, concerns and problems that started during preschool years might become more complex as a result of the fact that the child might assume guilt, blame, or responsibility for the parents' divorce, or by the child holding on to the improbable belief that he or she can bring the parents back together.

Five types of support that children of divorced parents need have been listed by Wolchik, Sandler, Braver, and Fogas (1989). These researchers have identified the following:

recreational, advice-giving, resource, emotional, and positive feedback. Emotional security that is gained from these types of supports are a significant factor in reducing risk for developing adjustment problems. In comparing the research related to boys and girls in terms of adjustment it is interesting to note both genders experience effects of divorce, but there are not as many differences as one might think. Both, boys and girls experience frustration and distress form emotional upset, worry, guilt, shame, doubting the quality of relationships with their parents and defending the absent parent. These upset reactions of hurt, anger, or general distress was found to be present and common in both boys and girls (Clarke-Stewart, et al., 2000; Koerner et al., 2004; Orbuch, 2000, Santrock, 1972). Boys and girls are both equally vulnerable when parents' divorce (Sun, 2001). The differences are found more in how they express their emotional feelings and this is impacted by social learning.

It could also be seen from the critical literature review that preventative intervention strategies should include the primary focus on parents and parenting practices. This is because disruptions in parenting practices are related to problems in child behaviors and maladjustment during family transitions. This is especially true in the mother and son relationship, once parents are divorced. A son often will feel the responsibility of being the man of the house and the need to help his mother financially. The burden upon the son only adds more stress to an already stressful situation, and often leads boys to defy their mothers, which results in negative outcomes. Pre-divorce programs that work with parents, especially mothers need to address parenting practices and the needs of families in unique structures and assist in bringing about a change in children's, especially boys' post-divorce maladjustment behaviors. During the adolescent year, effective parenting skills are needed to deter the development of more serious problems as the boy reaches adulthood, e.g. antisocial personality disorders, involvement in illegal activities, and the possibility of becoming incarcerated.

Conclusions, Recommendations, Contribution of New Knowledge

Modified Diathesis-Stress Model

Nevid, Rathus, & Greene (2003), among others, proposed the use of the psychological diathesis-stress model for assessing stress from risk factors. According to the model, disorders arise from a combination or interaction of a diathesis (vulnerability or predisposition) with stress. The model stipulates that behavior is a result of both life experiences (called nurture experiences) and genetic and biological factors (that are called nature factors). According to this model, mental disorders are produced by the interaction of some vulnerability characteristic, or predisposition, and a precipitating even in the environment (Emck, 1996). In other words, psychological problems are the result of stress affecting a person who has a pre-existing vulnerability or risk factor for developing a specific kind of problem. The proposed model could be used with protective and risk factors as a perspective for determining possible problematic behaviors and maladjustment in boys ages 8 through 12 whose families have experienced divorce. These maladaptive behaviors, when left untreated with no intervention could lead to the development of disorders and psychopathology, which may follow the adolescent into adulthood.

Modified Diathesis-Stress Model with Protective / Risk Factors

The proposed model is in part a modification of the investigative study conducted by Emck (1996). Emck (1996) used the diathesis-stress mode to teach patients to manage stress, in order to prevent a relapse in psychosis- in this case, schizophrenia. It could also be used to teach boys to manage stress after a divorce occurrence as well. The mode for Emck (1996) also became a useful tool for psycho-motor therapy for the purpose of structuring activities and interventions. Emck applied the mode for use in identifying the vulnerability of patients that allowed the symptoms of schizophrenia to develop. He then used this model for treatment purposes.

In considering the model with modifications related to boys' ages 8 to 12 whose parents have experienced divorce, the first step would be to look at the diathesis, which is defined as a psychological vulnerability (this does not have to be genetic). In applying this to parental divorce there are many types of vulnerabilities that could apply e.g. parental loss, guilt feelings of responsibility for the parent leaving. Second, it is necessary to identify that the stress factors are potential or real. These factors identify or are related to situational, environmental, or sociocultural stress factors e.g. family conflict, trauma, significant life changes, economic status, and parental discipline.

Protective and risk factors can divided into both positive and negative ways e.g. defense mechanisms, coping mechanisms, and social supports. Humans use coping and defense mechanisms to protect themselves, but when used ineffectively they can place a persona at greater risk. Many of the defense mechanisms can be utilized in a positive and negative form, e.g. repression, sublimation, rationalization, etc. Coping mechanisms are used to describe a collection of overt and covert strategies use during confrontation with challenges. These mechanisms include problem-solving skills and responses, gathering information, considering alternatives and consequences, communication behaviors, making a decision related to the best course of action.

Cognitive abilities in the proposed model as applicable to boys' 8-12 may include minimizing stress, focusing on positive aspects of a situation, and self-control. All of these protective and risk factors are impacted by the person's explanatory style of optimism or pessimism. According to Wills, Blechman, and McNamara (1996) affective challenges test an adolescent's capacity to recognize unpleasant facts and to achieve emotional balance throughout all types of life events. Young people with competence are more likely to control and rebound from emotional setbacks relatively quickly. The ability of people especially adolescent's to utilize these protective/risk factor dimensions may increase or decrease their abilities of adaptation. Hetherington and Blechman (1996) found effective strategies succeed in the short and long term by enhancing a positive or optimistic attitude about one's personal attributes and coping abilities.

It is more effective in the removal of the problematic situation. On the other hand, when ineffective strategies fail leaving the person alienated from supporters, the person's responses are met with an attitude of helplessness, leading to the development of a negative and pessimistic attitude about oneself. Further ineffective coping may lead to avoidance, venting of anger, and blaming and criticizing others in a negative manner. Seligman's (1992) studies have provided evidence that one's explanatory style impacts physical health and stress, which he refers to as habits of the heart. Further investigations are needed in addressing the possible impacts of the explanatory style relating to coping and defense mechanisms. With these further investigations, the field of psychology may be able to shed light upon why some people adapt and cope better to stressful traumatic situations and other people demonstrate behavioral problems and psychopathology leading to antisocial personality types.

The Modified Diathesis-Stress Model with protective/ risk factors postulates that an individual's internal and external factors being either positive or negative added together with one's explanatory style leads to adaption or maladjustment. This combination impacts the personality and a person's tendency toward protective (positive) factors or risk (negative) factors. When the person tends to utilize the protective (positive) factors the end result creates adaptation linking to resiliency. The reversal occurs when a person tends to utilize the risk (negative) factors the end result creates behavioral problems and disorders which often are linked to the antisocial personality.

Figure 3.1

Modified Diathesis-Stress Model with Protective/Risk Factors and Coping Strategies.

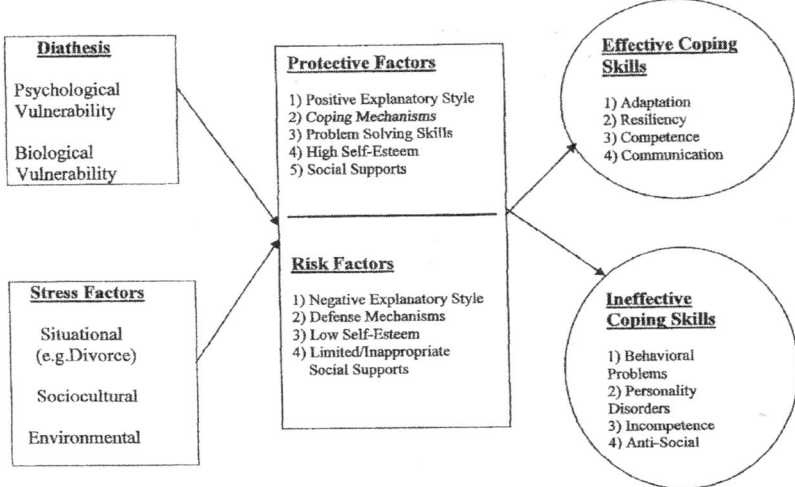

Modified Diathesis-Stress Model

The modified model not only is useful in the case of divorce effects related to boys, but may well be applicable to several areas of psychology. However, the following example provided in the summary may provide a more vivid explanation of the model. The modified model is demonstrated in the following summary.

Summary

An example, a young boy 8-12 years of age, experiences a secure attachment and bonding with his parents during infancy. He progresses through the developmental stages with little conflict. In infancy he built a trusting relationship with his parents and the environment. During the stages of industry and identity the young boy has become a more interactive participant within the environment. His foundation of trust has increased and he now interacts within the environment. His foundation of trust has increased and he now interacts with other individuals and seeks to be accepted by his peers. His self-worth and strong sense of self and a solid identity develop through his own learning, accomplishments, and interactions with others by means of recognition, competence, and praise. As the young boy confronts each stage of development and resolves the conflict he gains resiliency through the struggle. This resilience along with his explanatory style has positive tendencies along with a positive self-concept. These attributes will help lead him to acquire the protective factors needed for good solid coping and problem-solving skills when faced with a traumatic event or challenge (e.g. divorce of parents). These protective measures may include but are not limited to a positive explanatory style of thinking, effective coping, and problem solving skills provide him with the adequate means in facing this adverse challenge. This young adolescent has a good self-esteem and his appropriate social supports may include: aunts, uncles, grandparents, family friends, minister, teachers, counselors, and even siblings add to his self-worth and feelings of support and competency. These feelings added to his appropriate social supports provide the adolescent with the ability for positive adaptation and resiliency. The positive successful growth from the adverse event leads to adaptation, while it enhances and creates a more resilient human being. His resilience along with the positive explanatory style and all he has acquired up to this point in his life will continue to follow him throughout the life span.

The reverse would be true of a young boy from an insecure attachment and bonding with his parents. He would progress through the developmental stages with unresolved conflict and increased anxiety. He would have a weak foundation with a lack of trust relating to his parents and his environment. His explanatory style would be more negative with tendencies to lean toward the risk factors including a low self-esteem with an incompetent feeling, placing him at risk or more prone to utilize defense mechanisms, ineffective coping & problem solving skills, and the inability to communicate effectively with others. These risk factors would inhibit his ability to meet adverse events, creating more stress, anxiety, and aggression. These emotional feelings may build up in the boy creating the pressure cooker effect. These interactions may lead to behavioral problems, depression, suicidal ideation, no self-worth, blaming of others, juvenile delinquency, drug & alcohol abuse, illegal activities, deviant sexual conduct. Without professional intervention to correct these unresolved conflicts, the young boy's life may spin out of control and the behavioral problems may continue to escalate leading to a dangerous antisocial personality or other type of psychopathology. These are many of the characteristics seen today in young individuals involved with the legal system and a good example would be the Columbine tragedy.

Conclusion

The modified model in working with people may be helpful for professionals to assist them in assessing protective/ risk factors of boys ages 8-12 who have experienced a divorce situation in the immediate family- risk factors that lead to behavioral problems and maladjustment. Thus the study makes a meaningful contribution to social change in that it provides new information and a new way to treat maladaptive behavior of boys at this developmental age.

The prevention of utilizing ineffective coping skills and defense mechanisms could also serve to guide people, especially adolescents to a more positive, healthy, and optimistic outcomes in life. By using the modified model, professionals could assist in the prevention of negative outcomes from following adolescents into adulthood. By preventing ineffective coping and defense mechanisms that create problematic behaviors and psychopathology, a healthy adult lifestyle would be achieved. The contribution of this study is general and of the model, specifically, is thus clear.

Implications for social Change and Future Research Questions

The current modified diathesis-stress model can be used to assist boy boys and girls of divorce with more effective coping interventions, which help in the promotion of resiliency. The modified model has the potential to be most useful as an intervention model. Intervention could include, but not limited to pre-divorce or pre-marital counseling sessions for adults, post-traumatic stress syndrome from war veterans, school counseling for troubled youth, and psychological distress. Other implications of the modified model may include the use with all cultural populations, with no bias towards socioeconomic, age, gender, sex, religion, or sexual preference. The modified model could be utilized by therapists from all schools of psychology, especially in different types of counseling and therapy sessions with the possibility as a therapeutic intervention assessment tool. The modified model would be useful in the areas of Developmental, Personality, Marriage & Family, Sexuality, Abnormal, and Health Psychology. The possibilities provided by the current modified model are endless with implications for the promotion of resiliency and the deterrence of psychopathology.

Future research is strongly suggested with endless questions needing answered. Some question may include: Are there really gender differences relating to the effects of divorce on children? How does divorce impact children from non-traditional families e.g. gay, lesbian, transsexual, and bisexual? Does divorce effect children's sexuality? Are there adjustment issues for children from non-traditional families e.g. transsexual, bisexual, or gays? If there are what are the issues or adjustment problems? How much does stress and health issues impact children of divorce? How children from divorce-once grown, related to their own children? Are there differences in mother's and father's relationships with their children if they came from a divorced family? Further areas may include comparison studies of young children and older children's attitudes about divorce, parents, and adjustment to stressful life events, death & dying, etc. These are but a few of the many questions remaining and further research is needed in all of these areas.

During the past 25-35 years in which divorce has evolved, the continuum has gone from one extreme of the single mother households to single father households. What are the effects of divorce on children that have lived in father headed households with the mother as the absent parent? It is important to continue to monitor divorce effects separately for boys and girls, with both receiving equal attention. It is hard to believe there are really that many differences in how boys and girls adjustment is so different. This researcher does not believe there are as many differences between boys and girls adjustment, but in how these adolescence react to the upheaval in their lives, the changes that divorce creates for them, and the societal constraints placed upon them impacts them differently to varying degrees.

Amato, P. R. (1993). Children's adjustment to divorce: Theories, hypotheses, and empirical support. *Journal of Marriage and Family, 55,* 23-28.

Amato, P. R., & Keith, B. (1991). Parental divorce and the well-being of children: A meta-analysis. *Psychological Bulletin, 110,* 26-46.

Ainsworth, M. D. (1973).The development of infant-mother attachment. In B. Caldwell & H. Ricchiuto (Eds.). *Review of Child Development Research 3,* IL: University of Chicago Press.

Ainsworth, M. D., & Bell, S. M. (1969). Some contemporary patterns of mother-infant interaction in the feeding situation. In J. A. Ambrose (Ed.). *Stimulation in Early Infancy.* London: Academic.

Ainsworth, M. D. S., Blehar, M. C., Waters, E., & Wall, S. (1978). *Patterns of attachment: A psychological study of the strange situation.* NJ: Erlbaum.

Alexander, J. F., Waldron, H. B., Barton, C., & Mas, C. H. (1989). The minimizing of blaming attributions and behaviors in delinquent families. *Journal of Consulting and Clinical Psychology, 57,* 19-24.

Allen, J. P., & Bell, K. L. (1995 March). *Attachment and communication with parents and peers in adolescence.* Paper presented at the biennial meetings of the Society for Research in Child Development, Indianapolis, IN.

Allen, J. P., Hauser, S. T., O'Connor, T. G., Bell, K. L., & Eickholt, C. (1996). The connections of observed hostile family conflict to adolescents' developing autonomy and relatedness with parents. *Development and Psychopathology, 8,* 425-442.

Bandura, A. (1977). *Social learning theory.* NJ: Prentice-Hall.

Bandura, A. (1982). Self-efficacy mechanisms in human agency. *American psychologist, 37,* 122-147.

Barrera, M. (1981). Social support's role in adjustment of pregnant adolescents: Assessment issues and findings. In B. H. Gotteib (Ed.). *Social networks and social support in community mental health.* (pp. 69-96). Beverly Hills, CA: Sage.

Baum, A., Gatchel, R. J., & Krantz, D. S. (1997). *An introduction to health psychology.* (3rd Ed.). Boston, MA: McGraw-Hill.

Beautrais, A. L., Fergusson, D. M., & Shannon, F. T. (1982). Life events and childhood morbidity: A prospective study. *Pediatrics, 70,* 935-940.

Biller, H. (1981). Father absence, divorce and personality development. In M. Lamb (Ed.). *The role of the father in child development* (2nd Ed.). pp. 489-522. New York: John Wiley.

Booth, A., & Amato, P. R. (1994). Parental marital quality, parental divorce, and relations with parents. *Journal of Marriage and Family, 56,* 21-34.

Bowlby, J. (1958). The nature of the child's tie to his mother. *Psychoanalysis, 39*, 35.

Bowlby, J. (1969). *Attachment and loss.* New York: Basic Books.

Bowlby, J. (1973). *Separation and loss.* New York: Basic Books.

Bowlby, J. (1980). *Attachment and loss.* Vol. 3: Loss, sadness and depression. New York: Basic Books.

Boyce, T. W., Jensen, E. W., Cassell, J. C., Collier, A. M., Smith, A. H., & Raimey, C. T. (1973). Influence of life events and family routines on childhood respiratory tract illness. *Pediatrics, 60*, 609-615.

Bretherton, I., & Walters, E. (1990). Attachment theory: Retrospect and prospect; growing points of attachment theory and research. *Monographs of the Society for Research in Child Development, 50* (Serial No. 20a).

Brofenbrenner, U. (1979). *The ecology of human development.* MA: Harvard University Press.

Brofenbrenner, U. (1986). Ecology of the family as a context for human development: Research Perspectives. *Developmental Psychology, 22*, 723-742.

Burns, M., & Seligman, M. E. (1989). Explanatory style across the lifespan: Evidence for stability. *Journal of Personality and Social Psychology, 56*, 471-477.

Caldwell, B. M., Wright, C. M., Honig, R., & Tannenbaum, J. (1970). Infant day care and attachment. *American Journal of Orthopsychiatry, 40*, 397-412.

Capaldi, D. M. & Patterson, G. R. (1991). Relation of parental transitions to boys' adjustment problems: I. A linear hypothesis. II. Mothers at risk for transitions and unskilled parenting. *Developmental Psychology, 3*, 489-504.

Carlson, V., Cicchetti, D., Barnett, D., & Braunwald, K. G. (1989). Finding order in disorganization: Lessons from research on maltreated infants' attachments to their caregivers. In D. Cicchetti & V. Carlson (Eds.), *Child Maltreatment* (pp. 494-528). Cambridge: Cambridge University Press.

Cherlin, A. J., Furstenberg, F. F., Chase-Lansdale, P. L., Kiernan, K. E., Tobins, P. K., Morrison, D. R., & Teitler, J. O. (1991). Longitudinal studies of effects of divorce on Children in Great Britain and the United States. *Science, 252*, 1386-1389.

Clarke-Stewart, K. A., Vandell, D. L., McCartney, K., Owen, M. T., & Booth, C. (2000). Effects of parental separation and divorce on very young children. *Journal of Family Psychology, 14*, 304-326.

Creswell, J. W. (2003). *Research design, qualitative, quantitative, and mixed methods approaches.* (2nd Ed.). Thousand Oaks, CA: Sage.

Crittenden, P. M. (1981). Abusing, neglecting, problematic and adequate dyads: Differentiating by patterns of interaction. *Merrill Palmer Quarterly, 27*, 1-18.

Crittenden, P. M. (1988). Relationships at risk. In J. Belsky & T. Nezworski (Eds.), *Clinical Implications of Attachment* (pp. 136-174). NJ: Erlbaum.

Crittenden, P. M. (1990). Internal representational models of attachment relationships. *Infant Mental Health Journal, 11*, 259-277.

Cicchetti, D. & Toth, S. L. (1996a). Patterns of relatedness, depressive symptomatology, and perceived competence in maltreated children. *Journal of Consulting and Clinical Psychology, 64*, 32-41.

Cicchetti, D. & Toth, S. L. (1996b). The impact of relatedness with mother on school functioning in competence in maltreated children. *Journal of School Psychology, 34*, 247-266.

Coddington, R. D., & Troxell, J. R. (1980). The effect of emotional factors on football injury rates: A pilot study. *Journal of Human Stress, 6*, 3-5.

Cohen-Sadler, R., Berman, A. L., & King, R. A. (1982). Life stress and symptomatology: Determinants of suicidal behavior in children. *Journal of the American Academy of Child Psychiatry, 21*, 178-186.

Denham, S. A. (1998). *Emotional development in young children.* NY: Guilford Press.

Emck, C. (1996). Psychomotor therapy for adolescents with psychotic disorders: A diatheses stress approach. Paper read at the 1st European Congress for Psychomotor Activity "Psychomotor Activity and Human Development" in Marburg, Germany, September 19-21.

Emery, R., Hetherington, E., & DiLalla, L. (1984). Divorce, children, and social policy. In H. Stevenson & A. Siegel (Eds.). *Child development research and social policy, 1*, 189-266. Chicago: University of Chicago Press.

Emery, R. E., & O'Leary, K. D. (1982). Children's perceptions of marital discord and behavior problems of boys and girls. *Journal of Abnormal Child Psychology 10(1)*, 11-24.

Erikson, B. M. (1998). *Longing for dad: Father loss and its impact.* FL: Health Communications, Inc.

Erikson, E. H. (1980). *Identity and the life cycle.* New York: W.W. Norton.

Erikson, E. H. (1959). Identity and the life cycle: Selected papers. *Psychological Issue Monograph Series I* (No. 1). New York: International Universities Press.

Erikson, E. H. (1968). *Identity: Youth and crisis.* New York: W. W. Norton.

Eysenck, M. W. (1982). *Attention and arousal: Cognition and performance.* New York: SpringerVerlag.

Fine, S. (1987). Children in divorce, custody, and access situations: An update. *Journal of Child Psychology and Psychiatry, 28*(3), 361-364.

Folkman, S., & Lazarus, R. S. (1980). An analysis of coping in a middle-aged sample. *Journal of Health and Social Behavior, 21,* 219-239.

Fonagy, P., Steele, H., & Steele, M. (1991). Maternal representations of attachment during Pregnancy predict the organization of infant-mother attachment at one year of age. *Child Development, 62,* 891-905.

Forman, S. G. (1993). *Coping skills interventions for children and adolescents.* San Francisco, CA: Jossey-Bass Publishers.

Forgatch, M. S., Patterson, G. R., Skinner, M. L. (1998). A mediational model for the effect of Divorce on antisocial behavior in boys. In E. M. Hetherington & J. D. Arestich (Eds.). *Impact of divorce, single parenting, and step-parenting on children* (pp. 135-154). Hillsdale, NJ: Lawrence Erlbaum Associates.

Gad, M. T., & Johnson, J. H. (1980). Correlates of adolescent life stress as related to race, sex, and levels of perceived social supports. *Journal of Clinical Child Psychology, 9,* 13-16.

Garvin, V., Leber, M. A., & Kalter, N. (1991). Children of divorce: Predictors of change following preventive intervention. *American Journal of Orthopsychiatry, 61*(3), 438-447.

Glick, P. C., & Lin, S. (1986). Recent changes in divorce and remarriage. *Journal of Marriage and Family, 48,* 737-747.

Goodman, M. P., Brunley, H. E., Schwartz, K. R., & Purcell, D. W. (1993). Gender and age in the relation between stress and children's school adjustment. *Journal of Early Adolescence, 13,* 329-345.00000

Greene, J. W., Walker, L. S., Hickson, G., & Thompson, J. (1985). Stressful life events and somatic complaints in adolescents. *Pediatrics, 75,* 19-22.

Greene, R. M., & Leslie, L. A. (1989). Mothers' behavior and sons' adjustment following divorce. *Journal of Divorce, 12,* 235-251.

Guidubaldi, J., & Perry, J. (1985). Divorce and mental health sequelae for children: A two-Year follow-up of a nationwide sample. *Journal of the American Academy of Child Psychiatry, 24,* 531-537.

Harlow, H. F., & Zimmerman, R. R. (1959). Affectional responses in the infant monkey. *Science, 130,* 421-432.

Heisel, J. S., Ream, S., Raitz, R., Rappaport, M., & Coddington, R. D. (1973). The significance of life events as contributing factors in the diseases of children. *Behavioral Pediatrics, 83,* 119-123.

Hetherington, E. M., & Blechman, E. A. (1996). *Stress, coping, and resiliency in children and families.* Mahwah, NJ: Lawrence Erlbaum Associates, Publishers.

Hetherington, E. M., Cox, M., & Cox, R. (1979). Play and social interaction in children following divorce. *Journal of Social Issues, 35,* 26-49.

Hetherington, E. M., & Parke, R. D. (1979). *Child psychology: A contemporary viewpoint.* (2nd Ed.). New York: McGraw-Hill Book Company.

Hodges, K., Kline, J. J., Barbero, G., & Flanery, R. (1984). Life events in the diseases of children with recurrent abdominal pain. *Journal of Psychosomatic Research, 28,* 185-188.

Hopf, S. M. (2010). Risk and resilience in children coping with parental divorce. Dartmouth Undergraduate Journal of Science, Spring 2010, Retrieved 2/16/2017 from:dujs. dartmouth.edu/.../**risk-and-resilience-in-children-coping-with-parental-divorce**#.WKY8V28rKM9.

Howell, S. H., Portes, P. R., & Brown, J. H. (1997). Gender and age differences in child adjustment to parental separation. *Journal of Divorce and Remarriage, 27,* 141-158.

Izard, C. E., Haynes, O. M., Chisholm, G., & Book, K. (1991). Emotional detriments of infant mother attachment. *Child Development, 62,* 906- 917.

Jacobs, T. J., & Charles, E. (1980). Life events and the occurrence of cancer in children. *Psychosomatic Medicine, 42,* 11-24.

Jenkins, J. M., & Smith, M. A. (1993). A prospective study of behavioral disturbance in children who subsequently experience parental divorce: A research note. *Journal of Divorce and Remarriage, 19,* 143-160.

Johnson, J. H. (1986). *Life events as stressors in childhood and adolescence.* Newbury Park, CA: Sage.

Johnson, J. H., & McCutcheon, S. (1980). Assessing life events in older children and adolescents: Preliminary findings with the life events checklist. In I. G. Sarason & C. D. Spielberger (Eds.), Stress and anxiety, 7, 111-125. Washington, D.C.: Hemisphere.

Kelly, J. B. (1993). Current research on children's post-divorce adjustment: No simple answers. *Family and Conciliation Courts Review, 31,* 29-49.

Kobak, R. R., Cole, H. E., Ferenz-Gillies, R., & Fleming, W. S. (1993). Attachment and emotion regulation during mother-teen problem solving: A control theory analysis. *Child Development, 64,* 231-245.

Lamb, M. E. (1981). The development of social expectations in the first year of life. In M. E. Lamb & L. Sherrod (Eds.), *Infant Social Cognition* (pp. 155-175). NJ: Erlbaum.

Lamb, M. E., Gaesenbauer, T. S., Malkin, C. M., & Schultz, L. A. (1985). The effects of abuse and neglect on security of infant-adult attachment. *Infant Behavior and Development, 8,* 35-45.

Lamb, M. E., Thompson, R. A., Gardner, W., & Charnov, E. L. (1985). *Infant-mother attachment: the origins and development significance of individual differences in strange situation behavior.* NJ: Erlbaum.

Lawrence, D. B., & Russ, S. W. (1985). *Mediating variables between life stress and symptoms among young adolescents.* Paper presented at the annual meeting of the American Psychological Association, Los Angeles, CA.

Lay, K. L., Waters, E., & Park, K. A. (1989). Maternal responsiveness and child compliance: The role of mood as mediator. *Child Development, 60,* 1405-1411.

Lazarus, R. S., & Launier, R. (1978). Stress-related transactions between persons and environment. In L. A. Pervin & M. Lewis (Eds.), *Perspectives in interactional psychology* (pp. 287-327). New York: Plenum.

Lefrancois, G. R. (1990). *The lifespan.* (3rd Ed.). Belmont, CA: Wadsworth.

Leaverton, D. R., White, C. A., McCormick, C. R., Smith, P., & Sheikholislam, B. (1980). Parental loss antecedent to childhood diabetes mellitus. *Journal of the American Academy of Child Psychiatry, 19,* 678-689.

Luthar, S. S., Burack, J. A., Cicchetti, D., & Weisz, J. R. (1997). *Developmental psychopathology: Perspectives on adjustment, risk, and disorder.* Melbourne, Australia: Cambridge University Press.

Lyons-Ruth, K., Alpern, L., & Repacholi, B. (1993). Disorganized infant attachment classification and maternal psychosocial problems as predictors of hostile-aggressive behavior in the preschool classroom. *Child Development, 64,* 572-585.

Lyons-Ruth, K., Connell, D. B., & Zoll, D. (1989). Patterns of maternal behavior among infants at risk for abuse: Relations with infant attachment behavior and infant development at 12 months of age. In D. Cicchetti, & V. Carlson (Eds.), *Child Maltreatment* (pp. 464-493). Cambridge: Cambridge University Press.

MacKinnon-Lewis, C., Lamb, M. E., Arbuckle, B., Baradaran, L. P. (1992). The relationship between biased maternal and filial attributions and the aggressiveness of their interactions. *Developmental & Psychopathology, 4,* 403-415.

Mahler, M. S., Pine, F., & Bergman, A. (1975). *The psychological birth of the human infant: Symbiosis and individuation.* New York: Basic Books.

Main, M., & Goldwyn, R. (in press). Adult attachment rating and classification systems. In M. Main (Eds.), *A typology of human attachment organization assessed in discourse drawings and interviews.* New York: Cambridge University Press.

Main, M., Kaplan, N., & Cassidy, J. (1985). Security in infancy, childhood, and adulthood: A move to the level of representation. In I. Bretherton & E. Waters (Eds.), Growing points in attachment theory and research (pp. 66-104). *Monographs of the Society for Research in Child Development, 50,* (Serial No. 209).

Main, M., & Solomon, J. (1986). Discovery of a new, insecure-disorganized/disoriented attachment pattern. In T. B. Brazelton & M. Yogman (Eds.), *Affective development in infancy* (pp. 95-124). NJ: Ablex.

Marcia, J. E. (1966). Development and validation of ego identity status. *Journal of Personality and social Psychology, 3*(5), 551-558.

Martinez, Jr., C. R., & Forgatch, M. S. (2002). Adjusting to change: Linking family structure transitions with parenting and boys' adjustment. *Journal of Family Psychology, 16,* 107-117.

Masten, A. S., Best, K. M., & Garmezy, N. (1990). Resilience and development: Contributions from the study of children who overcome adversity. *Development and Psychopathology, 2,* 435-444.

Meyer, R. J., & Haggerty, R. J. (1962). Streptococcal infections in families. *Pediatrics, 29,* 539-549.

Morrison, D. R., & Cherlin, A. J. (1995). The divorce process and young children's well-being: A prospective analysis. *Journal of Marriage and the Family, 57,* 800-812.

Mott, F L., Kowaleski-Jones, L., & Meneghan, E. G. (1997). Paternal absence and child behavior: Does a child's gender make a difference? *Journal of Marriage and the Family, 59,* 103-118.

Nevid, J. S., Rathus, S. A., & Greene, B. (2003). *Abnormal psychology in a changing world.* (5th Ed.). New Jersey: Prentice Hall.

Olweus, D. (1980). Familial and temperamental determinants of aggressive behavior in adolescent boys: A causal analysis. *Developmental Psychology, 16*(6), 644-660.

Orbuch, T. L., Thornton, A., Cancio, J. (2000). The impact of marital quality, divorce, and remarriage on the relationships between parents and their children. *Marriage & Family Review, 29,* 221-246.

Padilla, E. R., Rohesnow, D. J., & Bergman, A. B. (1976). Predicting accident frequency in children. *Pediatrics, 58,* 223-226.

Pantell, R. H., & Goodman, B. W. (1983). Adolescent chest pain: A prospective study. *Pediatrics, 71,* 881-886.

Patterson, J. M., & McCubbin, H. I. (1983). The impact of family life events and changes on the health of a chronically ill child: Family relations. *Journal of applied Family and Child Studies, 32,* 255-264.

Pearlin, L. I., & Schooler, C. (1978). The structure of coping. *Journal of Health and Social Behavior, 22,* 337-356.

Pervetti, P. O. & DiVitorrio, A. (1992). Effect of loss of father through divorce on personality of the preschool child. *Journal of Instructional Psychology, 19,* 269-273.

Peterson, C., Seligman, M. E. P., & Vaillant, G. E. (1988). Pessimistic explanatory style is a risk factor for physical illness: A thirty-five year longitudinal study. *Journal of Personality and Social Psychology, 55,* 23-27.

Rice, F. P. (2001). *Human development.* (4ᵗʰ Ed.). NJ: Prentice Hall.

Risks, M. H. (1985). Social transmission of parental behavior: Attachment across generations. In I. Bretherton & E. Waters (Eds.), Growing points of attachment theory and research (pp. 211-227). *Monographs of the Society for Research in Child Development. 49.*

Rodriguez, H., & Arnold, C. (1998). Children & divorce: A snapshot...Accessed on line December 28, 2000 at hettp://www.clasp.org/pubs/family/formation.

Rosenhan, D. L., & Seligman, M. E. P. (1984). *Abnormal psychology.* New York: W.W. Norton & Company, Inc.

Russo, D. C., Cataldo, M. F., & Cushing, P. J. (1981). Compliance training and behavioral covariation in the treatment of multiple behavior problems. *Journal of Applied Behavior Analysis, 14,* 209-222.

Rutter, M. (1987). Psychosocial resilience and protective mechanisms. *American Journal of Orthopsychiatry, 57,* 316-331.

Rutter, M. (1990). Psychosocial resilience and protective mechanisms. In J. Ralf, A. S. Matsen, D. Cicchetti, K. H. Nuechterlein, & S. Weintraub. (Eds.). *Risk and protective factors in the development of psychopathology* (pp. 181-214). New York: Cambridge University Press.

Sameroff, A. J., & Seifer, R. (1990). Early contributors to development risk. In J. Ralf, A.S. Masten, D. Cicchetti, K. H. Nuechterlein, & S. Weintraub. (Eds.). *Risk and protective factors in the development of psychopathology* (pp. 52-66). New York: Cambridge University Press.

Santrock J. W. (1972). Relation of type and onset of father absence to cognitive development. *Child Development, 43,* 455-470.

Santrock, J. W. (1975). Father absence, perceived maternal behavior, and moral development in boys. *Child Development, 46,* 753-757.

Schaffer, H. R., & Emerson, P. E. (1964). The development of social attachments in infancy. *Monographs of the Society for Research in Child Development, 29* (3) (Serial No. 94).

Schulman, P., Castellon, C., & Seligman, M. E. P. (1989). Assessing explanatory style: The content analysis of verbatim explanations and the attributional style questionnaire. *Behavior Research and Therapy, 27,* 505-512.

Sears, R. R., Maccoby, E. E., & Levin, H. (1975). *Patterns of child rearing.* New York: Harper & Row.

Seligman, M. E. P. (1992). *Learned optimism: How to change your mind and your life.* New York: Simon & Schuster, Inc.

Selye, H. (1976), *The stress of life.* (2nd Ed.). New York: McGraw-Hill.

Shaw, D. S., Emery, R. E., & Tuer, M. d. (1993). Parental functioning and children's adjustment in families of divorce: A prospective study. *Journal of Abnormal Child Psychology, 21*(1), 119-134.

Silverberg-Koerner, S., Wallace, S., Jacobs-Lehman, S., A. Lee, S., & Escalante, K. A. (2004). Sensative mother-to-adolescent disclosures after divorce: Is the experience of sons different from that of daughters? *Journal of Family Psychology, 18,* 45-57.

Simons, R. L. (1996). *Understand differences between divorced and intact families: Stress, interaction, and child outcome.* Thousand Oaks, CA: Sage.

Simons, R. L., Lin, K. H., Gordon, L. C., Conger, R.D., & Lorenz, F. O. (1999). Explaining the higher incidence of adjustment problems among children of divorce compared with those in two-parent families. *Journal of Marriage & the Family, 61*(4), 1020-1034.

Smith, M. S., Gad, M. T., & O'Grady, L. (1983). Psychosocial functioning, life change, and clinical status in adolescents with cystic fibrosis. *Journal of Adolescent Health Care, 4,* 230-234.

Solnit, A. J. (1984). Keynote address: Theoretical and practical aspects of risks and vulnerability in infancy. *Child Abuse and Neglect, 8,* 133-144.

Sroufe, L. A. (1982). Individual patterns of adaption from infancy to preschool. In M. Perlmutter (Eds.), *Development and policy concerning children with special needs: Minnesota symposium on child psychology.* NJ: Erlbaum.

Sroufe, L. A, Bennett, C., Englund, M., & Urban, J. (1993). The significance of gender boundaries in preadolescents: The contemporary correlates and antecedents of boundary violations and maintenance. *Child Development, 64,* 455-466.

Sroufe, L. A., & Fleeson, J. (1986). Attachment and the construction of relationships. In W.W. Hartup & Z. Rubin (Eds.), *Relationships and development* (pp. 51-71). NJ: Erlbaum.

Sroufe, L. A. Schork, E., Motti, E., Lawroski, N., & LaFreniere, P. (1984). The role of affect in emerging social competence. In C. Izard, J. Kagn, & R. Zajonc (Eds.), *Emotion, Cognition, and behavior* (pp. 289-319). New York: Cambridge University Press.

Stein, S. P., & Charles, E. (1971). Emotional factors in juvenile diabetes mellitus: A study of early life experiences of adolescent diabetics. *American Journal of Psychiatry, 128,* 56-60.

Strober, M. (1984). Stressful life events associated with bulimia in anorexia nervosa. *International Journal of Eating Disorders, 3,* 1-13.

Sun, Y. (2001). Family environment and adolescents' well-being and after parents' marital disruption: A longitudinal analysis. *Journal of Marriage and Family, 63,* 697-713.

Tunks, E., & Bellissimo, A. (1990). *Behavioral medicine: Concepts and procedures.* New York: Pergamon Press.

Wallerstein, J. S., & Blakeslee, S. (1989). *Second chances: Men, women, and children a decade after divorce.* New York: Ticknor & Fields.

Wallerstein, J. S., & Kelly, J. (1980). *Surviving the breakup: How children and parents cope with divorce.* New York: Basic Books.

Water, E., Wippman, J., & Sroufe, L. A. (1979). Attachment, positive affect, and competence in the peer group: Two studies in construct validation. *Child Development, 50,* 821-829.

Wills, T. A., Blechman, E. A., & McNamara, G. (1996). Family support, coping, and competence. In E. M. Hetherington & E. a. Blechman (Ed). *Stress, coping, and resiliency in children and families* (pp. 107-133). Mahwah, NJ: Lawrence Erlbaum Associates, Publishers.

Wolchik, S. A., Sandler, I. N., Braver, S. L., & Fogas, B. (1989). Events of parental divorce: Stressfulness ratings by children, parents, and clinicians. *American Journal of Community Psychology, 14,* 59-74.

Woodward, L., Fergusson, D. M., & Belsky, J. (2000). Timing of parental separation and attachment to parents in adolescence' results of a prospective study from birth to age 16. *Journal of Marriage & the Family, 62*(1), 162-173.

Zaslow, M. J. (1988). Sex differences in children's response to parental divorce: I. Research methodology and post-divorce family forms. *American Journal of Orthopsychiatry, 58,* 355-378.

Zill, N., Morrison, Dr. R., & Coiro, M. J. (1993). Long term effects of parental divorce on parent-child relationships, adjustment, and achievement in young adulthood. *Journal of Family Psychology, 7*(1), 93-103.

About the Author

Deborah Henady-Korba earned a bachelor's degree in psychology from Saint Joseph College in Rensselaer, Indiana, and a master's and PhD(ABD) in educational/clinical psychology from Walden University. She has been teaching psychology since 1999, currently at the Art Institute and the University of Phoenix. Deborah and her late husband, Jerome, made their home in Lafayette, Indiana. She has six children and twelve grandchildren.

Manufactured by Amazon.ca
Bolton, ON